the
DRAKENSBERG BUSHMEN
and THEIR ART

With a guide to the rock painting sites

A.R. WILLCOX
F.R.S. (S.A.), F.S.A., F.R.A.I.

Published by Drakensberg Publications
P.O. Box 26, Winterton 3340, Natal

ISBN 0 620 07419 1

First published 1984
Second impression 1985

CONTENTS

Page

Acknowledgements v
List of Figures vi
List of Black and White Plates vi
List of Colour Plates vii
Preface viii
Key Map xi

Section 1 — THE ARTISTS AND THE ART
1. The Setting 1
2. The Peopling of the 'Berg 3
3. The Bushman Way 15
4. The Animals of the 'Berg and
   the Paintings 37
5. The Painters' Materials and
   Technique 47
6. The Paintings as Art 49
7. A Bushman Cave 53
8. Some Problems 55

Section 2 — RESORTS
1. NATAL PARKS BOARD PARKS AND
   RESERVES (listed alphabetically) 60
   Giant's Castle Game Reserve 61
   Himeville Nature Reserve 61
   Injasuti Hutted Camp 61
   Kamberg Nature Reserve 62
   Loteni Nature Reserve 62
   Royal Natal National Park and
   Rugged Glen Nature Reserve 63
   Vergelegen Nature Reserve 63

2. FORESTRY STATIONS (listed alphabetically) 64
   Cathedral Peak 65
   Cobham 65
   Garden Castle 66
   High Moor 66
   Mkhomazi 67
   Monk's Cowl 67

3. HOTELS (Listed alphabetically) 68
   Bushman's Nek Hotel 68
   Cathedral Peak Hotel 69
   Cathkin Park Hotel 70
   Cavern Berg Resort 71
   Champagne Castle Hotel 71
   Drakensberg Gardens Hotel 72

El Mirador Hotel. 72
Himeville Hotel. 72
Hotel Walter, Bergville. 73
Little Switzerland Hotel. 73
Mont-aux Sources Hotel. 73
Nest Hotel 73
Royal Natal National Park Hotel. 74
Sani Pass 74
Underberg Hotel. 75
White Mountain Resort. 75

4. CARAVAN PARKS
Dragon Peaks. 76
Kelvin Grove 76
Mountain Splendour 77

Section 3 – ROCK PAINTING SITES
Bamboo Hollow. 78
Battle Cave. 78
Buy's Cave. 79
Christmas Cave 80
Eland Cave. 80
Elephant Cave 81
Game Pass Shelter. 81
Ikanti Hill 82
Junction Shelter. 82
Knuffel's Shelter. 83
Kranses, Kamberg Area 83
Ladder Shelter 84
Main Caves, Giant's Castle Game Reserve. 85
Mpongweni 86
Mushroom Hill Cave 87
Nuttall's Shelter. 88
Oliviershoek Shelter. 88
Sandra's Shelter. 89
Sebaaini Shelter. 89
Steel's Shelter. 90
Sunday Falls Shelter. 90
Willcox's Shelter. 90
Willem's Cave. 91
Xeni Shelter. 91

Section 4 – HINTS FOR PHOTOGRAPHERS. 92
Further Reading. 94
Index of Sites
Advertising Section
    Hotels
    Caravan Parks
    General

ACKNOWLEDGEMENTS

In revisiting the rock painting sites in their Reserves I have enjoyed the hospitality of the Natal Parks Board and have received the friendly co-operation of their Wardens and Rangers. The Department of Forestry officials in their areas have also been co-operative.

Some of the line drawings are 'after' Patricia Vinnicombe in her invaluable book **The People of the Eland** (see Further Reading).

My debt to artist Colin Nockels, who prepared all the figures and the map and advised on the layout, will be apparent to the reader. I am also much indebted to Mr Henry Hyde of Estcourt for encouragement and much good advice in preparing this work. But as usual my chief debt is to my wife for her company on the many strenuous walks, and for all the typing and retyping, and acting as secretary.

LIST OF FIGURES

                                                            Page

1. Bushman stone implements. 4
2. Bantu with their shields 8
3. Fat-tailed sheep 8
4. A trek, probably Gardener's. 9
5. The end of a cattle raid. 12
6. Bushmen and their clothing. 17
7. Steatopygous women with aprons. 17
8. Women with their equipment 19
9. Men and their equipment. 20
10. Women and food collecting equipment. 21
11. Bushmen's huts. . . . . 21 & 22
12. Wild bees and honey collecting 23
13. Bushmen's rope bridges. 24
14. Harpooning fish. 25
15. Hunter driving eland into ambush 25
16. Hunters wearing animal skins as disguise. 27
17. A hunter hunted 27
18. Bushman dances. 28
19. Creatures from Bushman mythology. 33
20. Creatures from Bushman mythology. 35
21. Creatures from Bushman mythology. 36
22. The antelope of the Drakensberg. 38
23. The antelope of the Drakensberg. 39
24. Perspective in the art 51
25. Expressiveness in the art 52

LIST OF BLACK AND WHITE PLATES

                                                            Page

1. Sunday Falls, Royal Natal National Park. Kaross clad figures probably Bantu 6
2. The Kranses, Kamberg Area. Procession of figures probably Bantu, also hunters with eland. 7
3. Steel's Shelter, Giant's Castle. Eland and mounted hunters. 10
4. Steel's Shelter, Giant's Castle. Mounted hunters and child's copy 10
5. Farmers pursuing Bushmen cattle raiders. 11
6. Mpongweni, Underberg District. Bushman cattle raid 13
7. Ikanti Mountain, Sani Pass. Bushmen on trek 14
8. Kalahari Bushman and his wife 15
9. Ncibidwane Valley, Giant's Castle. Kaross clad figures and eland 18
10. The Eland Cave, Cathkin Area. Eland, also running and seated figures 22
11. Sebaaini Shelter, Ndedema Valley. Hunters wearing animal skin disguise 26
12. Tabamyama, Giant's Castle. Male figures dancing. 29
13. Mpongweni, Underberg District. Group of dancers. 30
14. Battle Cave, Giant's Castle. Detail of the battle scene. 31

15. Battle Cave, Giant's Castle. Detail of the battle scene. 32
16. Battle Cave, Giant's Castle. Insect-like figures with an animal-headed dancer. 33
17. Mushroom Hill, Cathedral Peak Area. Figure part animal, part human. 34
18. Willem's Shelter, Kamberg Area. Galloping Hartebeeste. 37
19. Battle Cave, Giant's Castle. Leopard. 40
20. Battle Cave, Giant's Castle. Rhinos or bushpigs. 41
21. Bushpig Shelter, Giant's Castle. Bushpig, fight, and figures walking 41
22. Main Cave (Western), Giant's Castle. Snake probably python 42
23. Mpongweni, Underberg District. Eland and human figures. 43
24. Game Pass Shelter, Kamberg Area. Eland with human figures. 44
25. Knuffel's Shelter also called Rhebok Shelter, Cathedral Peak. Herd of rhebok 44
26. Baboon Cave, The Cavern, Mont-aux-Sources Area. Rhebok and doe. 45
27. Ikanti Mountain, Sani Pass. Pair of grey rhebuck. 45

LIST OF COLOUR PLATES
Commencing opposite page number 28

I.   Giant's Castle Game Reserve. View from hutted camp.
II.   The Eland Cave, Cathkin Area. The cave and the high 'Berg.
III.   The Eland Cave, Cathkin Area. Many eland, also roan antelope and human figures.
IV.   Kamberg Nature Reserve. Eland herd.
V.   Battle Cave, Giant's Castle Game Reserve. The battle scene.
VI.   Socerers Shelter, Ndedema Gorge. Mythical creature, also buck and a crane.
VII.   Xeni Stream, Cathedral Peak Area. A rhebuck, bushbuck and group of Bushmen.
VIII.   Main Cave, Giant's Castle Game Reserve. Hunters, a feline and other figures.
IX.   Willcox's Shelter, Giant's Castle Game Reserve. Mythical creature.
X.   Game Pass Shelter, Kamberg Area. Eland, cloaked figures and tiny running figures.
XI.   Sandra's Shelter, Kamberg Area. Black-backed jackal howling.
XII.   Nuttall's Shelter, Kamberg Area. A reedbuck.
XIII.   Ulonyama, Kamberg Area. Dancers in a circle.
XIV.   Mpongweni, Underberg District. Group of Dancers.
XV.   Nuttall's Shelter, Kamberg Area. A pig hunt.
XVI.   The Meads, Griqualand East. Eland in various attitudes.

LIST OF ADVERTISERS

PREFACE

What is said in this little book is addressed to you, the visitor to the Drakensberg — Dragon Mountains — of Natal, by one who — now a resident — was for a great many years also a regular visitor and who can therefore anticipate their impact upon you.

Firstly, of course, the scenic grandeur, then the many sporting activities to be enjoyed in the (generally) delightful climate; and observation of the abundant wild life, the animals, the astonishing variety of birds and wild flowers.

All this you know, or soon will, but you might not know that the 'Berg is a vast open air museum of prehistoric man where until a bare century ago the Stone Age way of life persisted. Not might you realise that prehistoric rock art exists here in quantity unequalled elsewhere in the World in a equivalent area; and in artistic quality unrivalled, in some respects, even by the Palaeolithic rock art of Europe, even by the masterpieces of Lascaux and Altamira; and unlike them easily accessible to the public.

As you do become aware of this, the usual questions will arise in your mind as they did in mine. Who were here before you to leave their art and other relics? When did they come and when depart? What their manner of living? The answers we have will be briefly given.

Apart from possible incursions by still earlier people the Stone Age inhabitants of the Drakensberg region were the people given the name 'San' by the Hottentots and 'Bushman' by the White man. If they had any general name for themselves we do not know it.

The Bushmen, alas, are no longer there, but thanks to them — for centuries they kept out the Black and then the White pastoralists and farmers — and the wisdom of the authorities who took control, huge areas of their territory are just as the last of the little yellow hunters left them. Most of the animals they hunted are stil there; so are the plants which also provided a large part of their food. You can, with some exertion, enjoyable in itself, see what they saw, shelter in their homes, feel the strain of a good climb where they trod before you, breathe air and drink mountain water as pure as they did. Where else in the World is this true of the hunting grounds of a vanished race? To get, as it were, into the sandals of the Bushmen in these surroundings can be a spiritual experience and you are helped to do this — to see the world indeed through their eyes — by the pictures they left on the rock. The paintings tell you what was important to the artists' community, what they enjoyed doing, what they liked to see. Some this will be apparent to any observer and the art can be enjoyed simply as such, but the pleasure can be increased by the knowledge necessary to interpretation. This it is my aim to pass on.

You might, as I did, become addicted to the study and, if so, want to make your own collection of photographs of the rock paintings and their setting. Some hints are appended which I hope will be useful, at least to the beginner.

In Section 2 of the book the rock art sites are listed which are easily accessible to the average walker, or rider, from each 'Berg resort, whether hotel, caravan park, camp site or accommodation provided by the Natal Parks Board at their reserves. Also information is given how to proceed to the sites: whether a guide or a map is available or whether you should ask for directions. Indications of the size of the 'picture gallery', the state of preservation of the paintings and the special interest of some of them, will also be given.

I shall describe the kinds of paintings which you may see, the scenes of action, the various animals depicted, and the strange creatures of the imagination, but to attempt anything like a complete guide with a catalogue of all individual paintings is quite impossible. It would require many large and expensive books. There are about 500 sites in the Drakensberg with from a single painting to several hundred in each. Well over 20 000 individual figures have been counted. Very few of the art sites has been recorded *in toto* as they should be by photography and traced copies. Here is a field in which the amateur still makes a useful contribution especially if he is an artist or a photographer or is willing to make a **statistical** study of the occurrence of the various elements in the art, and of how they are distributed over the region. There are many problems currently under discussion by the specialists concerning the interpretation and *raison d'etre* of the art, and the motives of the artists. These will be mentioned, with evidence for and against the various theories, and you are invited to ponder them, preferably in the painted caves.

It follows from what has been said above that your best use of the guide depends on whether you have already an interest in archaeology, and rock art in particular, and wish to see more of it; or whether it is for you a new interest aroused by a visit to one of the 'Berg resorts. In the first case, a perusal of Section 2 — The Resorts will enable you to choose those from which you can visit a few, or many, painted caves, with much or little walking, with or without a person to conduct you; and to learn which are the principal galleries. In the second case turn in Section 2 to the name of the resort at which you are staying, under which are mentioned the sites near by, what you may see there, and the arangements to direct or conduct you to them.

To avoid repetition of site descriptions under the names of more than one resort certain of the painted shelters and all the larger ones, and the more interesting-art in them, are described in Section 3.

Whether rock art is an established, or a new interest of yours I hope you will digest Section 2 **before** you go out.

Above all do nothing to damage the paintings This kind of art can never be created again; there are few hunter-gatherers left on earth and they are strongly influenced by alien modern cultures: what is left belongs to the World and to future generations as well as this. Do not be tempted to dampen, even with a fine spay, the paintings to make them clearer to see or photograph: this certainly does harm. And do not light a fire in a painted shelter. I think it is not necessary to say to anyone who will read this book, do not write your name on the rock, or leave litter. Leave nothing in fact, but your footprints to show that you have been there, and take nothing away that you did not bring.

If you and friends go painting-hunting on your own take warning: these smiling mountains can quickly frown and mist roll down to reduce visibility to a few yards. Violent storms can come up out of only blue sky within an hour or two. After a hot day it can snow the next. I have myself been caught this way and I habitually take my rucksack with a raincoat, jerseys, and food in it even for a one-day walk. Never go alone for more than a short walk and let the personel at the hotel, reserve, or camp know where you are going. Preferably take a map with you. To include local maps centered on all the Drakensberg resorts would have greatly — and unnecessarily — increased the cost of this guide, so only a key map is given. Most hotels and reserves sell local maps very cheaply. Maps of the Government 1:50 000 Topographical Series cover the whole region and are obtainable from various bookshops and map offices, or direct from the Government Printer, Pretoria: but the most useful general map, which the visitor is urged to acquire, is that compiled by the Directorate of Forestry of the Department of Environmental Affairs. It is 1:50 000, in several sheets, coloured, and with contours at 20 metre intervals. The major footpaths are shown, also the caves on Forestry Reserves in which overnight camping is permitted. The map is obtainable from the offices of the Department and at most of its Reserves: also from some bookshops. It will be referred to later, in Section 2 (b), under the heading 'Forestry Stations'.

A two or three day hike through this wilderness is an experience — for the fit — not to be missed.

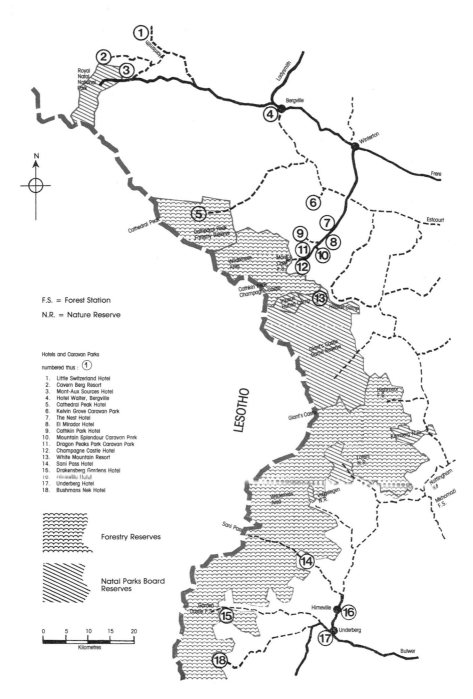

THE ARTISTS AND THE ART

1. THE SETTING

From your hotel or camp look up at the mountains *(colour plate I)*. At the top of the escarpment you will see dark rock in irregular masses visible in some parts for a height of hundreds of metres. This is basalt, a remnant of the vast flow of lava which once covered most of Southern Africa and the adjoining lands to the east and west. Near its base is a plateau of varying width — part of an ancient land surface — forming the top of what is called the Little Drakensberg or Little 'Berg. Immediately below this are exposed horizontal strata of light coloured rock, ranging from yellow to grey, called Cave Sandstone because of its manner of weathering to form overhangs — rock shelters *(colour plate II)*. Below the base of the Cave Sandstone there is usually a steep and well vegetated slope which conceals sandstones, shales and mudstones named the Red Beds and Molteno Beds. The lowest rocks you will find exposed in the 'Berg are other sandstones and shales of the Beaufort Series.

Dolerite 'dykes' cut through all these sedimentary beds and the rock is commonly visible extending in long lines marking the ancient fissures, or in isolated caps.

It is in the Cave Sandstone beds, and in huge lumps of it which have detached themselves and rolled down to lower levels, that most of the rock shelters are to be found in which the Bushmen lived and painted, firstly because they were the best shelters, but also, no doubt, because the light coloured, fine grained, rock provided the best 'canvasses' for the paintings. But there are some painted shelters in exposures of the lower beds. If you go hunting yourself for painting sites you might find a few under any overhang, but remember that the inhabited caves with sizable 'galleries' usually face north or east — the Bushmen liked sun, especially in the mornings — and have a fair amount of level floor, not too steep an approach, and water hard by. New sites with a few paintings are still being discovered, but it is safe to say that the large painted shelters are all known.

In spite of the convenient rock shelters, perennial streams, abundance of game and plant foods, and wood for fuel and making weapons and tools, one other requirement was necessary to Stone Age Man. It was, of course, stone suitable for making arrow heads, implements for cutting and shaping wood, for cutting up kills, scraping and cutting leather, and other household uses. The basalt, sandstones, and mudstones, and the dolerite, are useless for these purposes but Nature has met the need in two ways. In the lava as it cooled expanding gasses formed hollows and these were very slowly filled by silicious material carried in solution to form chalcedony, agate and similar hard stone which can be worked, with the necessary skill, to desired shapes,

1

and which take a sharp edge. Lumps of these stones weather out of the basalt and are to be found lying about or as pebbles in the streams. The second source of suitable stone for tools is where the molten magma of the basalt and dolerite welled up through the soft rock and by great heat and pressure converted some of it to 'indurated shale', also called lydianite or hornfels. It is dark, almost black in colour, flakes predictably, and is found in larger pieces than the silicious stones.

We need not, for our purposes, go further into the geology of the region but for those who wish to do so a publication is listed under King in 'Further reading' at the end of this book.

But you might like to contemplate as you climb from the base of the foothills to the top of the 'Little 'Berg' the fact that during that hour or two you are ascending through sixty million years of geological time from before 200 million years ago for the top of the Beaufort to about 150 million years when the lava began to flow. Your companions on the way are many small fossil dinosaurs at the Molteno and Red Bed levels persisting into the Cave Sandstone until the desert conditions indicated by the vast quantities of windblown sand that formed this rock eventually killed them off locally. At this level a few primitive fellow mammals will be with you. The great lava flows of the basalt extinguished all life over the region for many millions of years.

2. THE PEOPLING OF THE 'BERG

When the Natal interior first became known to European travellers the only people found to be living in the foothills and high ridges of the Drakensberg were the Bushmen, except perhaps for small numbers of Bantu fugitives from Chaka's impis hiding in the deep, well forested kloofs. How long the Bushmen had been there is a question for the archaeologist. Their stone implements, still to be found on the floors of their shelters and the slopes outside them, are all of the Late Stone Age, and the latter latter part of it, the tools being categorised as the Natal variation of the Smithfield complex of industries, simplified as 'Smithfield N'. Excavations have been made in the floor deposits of a dozen of the shelters down to the bed rock and with only two exceptions (and those very doubtful!) only Smithfield N Material has been found. In one other shelter material belonging to an earlier phase of the Later Stone Age was excavated and in two caves on the Lesotho side of the border Middle Stone Age implements were found in the archaeologists' 'digs', but neither of these kinds of stone artefacts can be linked to the Bushmen. It is certain that most of the rock paintings of the Drakensberg, and almost certainly all of them, were the work of the people who made the Smithfield N implements — and that these people were the Bushmen. The earliest date that can be given to these tools, therefore, will tell us also the age of the oldest rock paintings in the area.

Several radio-carbon dates are now available from layers containing Smithfield N material in rock shelters in the 'Berg. They range over approximately the last 2 000 years and on the evidence we now have we must assume that the rock paintings were executed over that period. Most of those still clearly visible no doubt were painted in the last few centuries.

How to recognise a manufactured stone tool? Firstly it will not be made of any of the 'Berg sandstones, which are useless for the purpose. Look for brought on material, the flint-like chert, hard silicous species which may be of various colours, and the dark, sometimes black indurated shale mentioned in Section 1:1. This might only be unworked material so next look for indications of working. The first step in making an inplement was usually to strike a flake off a 'core'. The blow produced a small bulb — the bulb of percussion — on the fracture surface of the flake, and a negative depression on the core. Concentric arcs may show below the bulb (fig 1). Then very small chips were removed from the edges to produce a tool for the purpose required — so look for worked edges. The core could also be further shaped as a tool.

Some typical artefacts are shown in the illustrations. The scrapers with one, two or three notches in them were used as spokeshaves for shaping bows, sticks and knobkerries. The tools sharpened at the end or along one side with a convex edge were for scraping skins to make clothing. Flakes with a straight sharp edge for cutting through animals' hides and cutting up the carcasses could take any forms. Probably they were often made at the kill and then discarded. Arrowheads were made of two small flakes cemented with a mastic to the shaft or fore-shaft or, more rarely, were beautifully made tanged points. Bone and iron points were also used. Tiny sharp points were used as augers for piercing skins, or shell to make beads. Another stone artefact was a flattened sphere with a hole through it which fitted over the sharp hardwood stick used by the women for digging up edible bulbs and roots, and was wedged tight. Only a few of these have been found in the 'Berg but they are fairly commonly shown in the paintings.

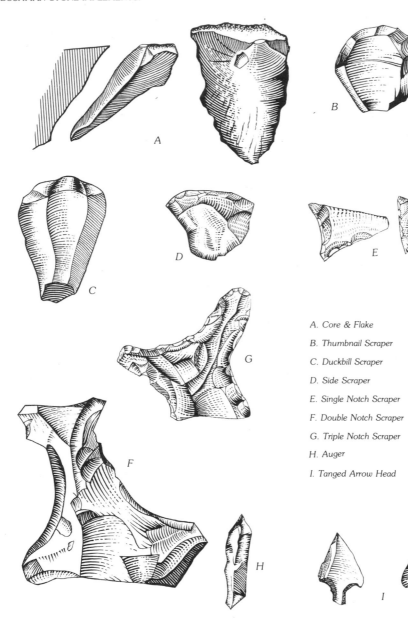

A. Core & Flake

B. Thumbnail Scraper

C. Duckbill Scraper

D. Side Scraper

E. Single Notch Scraper

F. Double Notch Scraper

G. Triple Notch Scraper

H. Auger

I. Tanged Arrow Head

Fig. 1

You may well find any of these stone implements if you look for them especially in the vicinity of the painted shelters. Photograph or sketch them if you will **but leave them exactly where they were found.** To remove or destroy any such artefact is an offence under the National Monuments Act of 1969, as amended, and carries heavy penalties; as also does damaging or removing any rock paintings.

We know from what is shown in many of the paintings — horses, guns and wagons for example — that the art continued to be practised well into the 19th Century and probably until the last of the artists were killed or driven over the wall of the Drakensberg into Lesotho about 1890.

There is evidence from other parts of South Africa for Later Stone Age cave dwellers and rock paintings much older than the beginning of our Era. You may ask why occupation of most of the 'Berg shelters was so late? Why did not the Middle Stone Age people live in them as they did elsewhere. The only plausible explanation is that the 'Berg above a certain level was too thickly forested for the hunters and their prey; and that the forests retreated only towards the end of Later Stone Age times. That the retreat was caused chiefly by the fires, mostly man-made, which still sweep through the mountains is suggested by the forest remnants which you will see on your walks. They are only on the south facing slopes, or in deep kloofs and gullys, where the ground and undergrowth remains damp enough to keep fires from penetrating. It licks at the edges, however, and prevents the patches from spreading. Without fire the whole 'Berg up to about 2 000 metres (6 560ft) would be forest.

The Bushmen once roamed over all Natal except other thickly forested areas, and were gradually forced back by newcomers with a way of life competing with theirs. These were the Iron Age people, the precursors of the so-called 'Bantu' tribes among whom the Zulus much later became dominant. They were small-scale agriculturalists but they needed large areas of grassland for the great herds of cattle on which their economy, indeed their whole social system, depended. As the number of Bantu and cattle increased, the Bushmen of Natal were pushed back by the more numerous and warlike new-comers as far as the slope of the Little 'Berg to join others of their race already in the Drakensberg. This must have caused some conflict over hunting rights and probably explains the rock paintings of fights between bands of Bushmen — normally peaceful among themselves.

The retreat to the mountains was affected by about the 14th Century. From radio-carbon dating we know there were Iron Age people in the Tugela Valley near the town of Weenen by the 7th Century. This is about 128 km (80 miles) from the Drakensberg. They were west of Estcourt by the 13th Century. The steep slope of the Little 'Berg formed the boundary between Bantu and Bushman territory for the next five centuries and this seems to have been accepted by both sides. Bantu, except as refugees, did not go beyond it, and Bushmen made only occasional hunting or cattle raiding forays into the Bantu lands, and quickly retreated. There is archaeological and historical evidence of trading and even some intermarriage between the two peoples.

The earliest **historical** account of Bantu being near the foothills of the 'Berg was by Portuguese survivors of the wrecked *Santo Alberto* when they encountered some near Richmond in 1593. They saw no Bushmen who were no doubt already confined to the mountains.

It is interesting to observe how much older in appearance the rock paintings outside the Little 'Berg boundary are compared with those within. From this fact alone the existence of a boundary for some centuries could be inferred. And as could be expected the kinds of paintings later to be evolved increase in frequency as the mountains are approached, reflecting the retreat of the artists.

One of the Bantu tribes in close contact with the Bushmen was the Amazizi who adopted the use of the bow and arrows from them — the only Bantu tribe in South Africa to do so. For this reason figures in the paintings shown with bows are not on this

Plate 1

Sunday Falls, Royal Natal National Park. Figures wearing karosses and with beads at the neck, knees and ankles. Probably representing Bantu.

6

ground alone necessarily Bushmen: other considerations must be taken into account, especially clothing worn, if any, and physical characteristics. The figures wearing long karosses and having grotesque prognathous heads, are no doubt Bantu, most likely Amazizi, even if carrying bows. But it is clear from the paintings that Bushmen in the 'Berg also wore the long kaross, as well as the shorter garment.

Plate 2

The Kranses, Kamberg Area. Procession of figures apparently carrying shields and therefore Bantu. Above, running figures and bichrome eland.

Knowledge of the approximate time of the Bantu approach to the mountains, and of what they brought with them, enables us to determine the maximum ages of some of the paintings — pictures of the Bantu themselves with their spears and shields *(fig 2)*; of their cattle, and of their sheep as they had these animals also, a hairy breed with very fat tails *(fig 3)*. The shape of the shields indicate the Bantu people depicted. The Zulu and related Nguni tribes, the Xhosa and AmaPondo, used the oval shields whilst that used by the BaSotho when they entered nearby territory had an indented hourglass shape. Bushmen, though they sometimes used a spear did not use shields, their fighting weapon being the bow which requires the use of both hands.

During the 1820's, the period when the Zulu king Chaka was subjugating the Bantu tribes of Natal, and dispossessed tribes were plundering others, some Bantu, bereft of their cattle and driven from their fields, hid in the deep kloofs and well screened rock shelters where some of their graves and fragments of their pottery have been found.

7

Tradition tells us that, in their desperation, they resorted to cannibalism. The Amazizi became notorious for this practice.

BANTU WITH SHIELDS

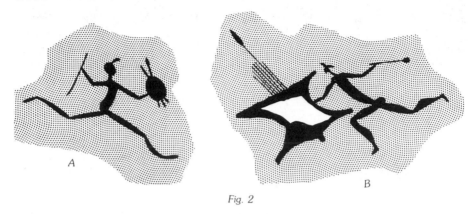

Fig. 2

A. Nguni. Underberg district   B. Basotho. Ongeluk's Nek.

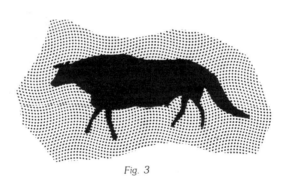

Fig. 3

Fat-tailed sheep. Ramatseliso Nek.

The white man was a late comer and his impact was quickly fatal to the Bushmen. In 1823 a settlement was made at Port Natal from which hunters and traders started to move inland. From 1829 traders, mainly after ivory, opened an overland route from the Cape via Grahamstown. The missionary Captain Allen Gardiner passed through the foothills near Underberg in 1835 and there is little doubt that it is his 'trek' with horses and a wagon that is depicted in a rock shelter there *(fig 4)*. The first horses seen in the region, hence the many rock paintings of them, date from this time onwards. The Bushmen stole horses in large numbers from the farmers and soon learnt to ride

8

Fig. 4   *Wagon with horsemen and cattle, probably Captain Allen Gardeners trek. Bamboo Mountain.*

and use them for hunting as the White men did, by running down their quarry until it was exhausted. There are some paintings showing this. Horses also provided meat when required 'on the hoof' and self-transporting.

The major White invasion of inland Natal was made by the Afrikaner Voortrekkers from 1837, and during the 1840's some of them started to occupy land under the 'Berg.

The Bushmen were now completely hemmed in as the highlands of Lesotho on the other side of the 'Berg were also being occupied by Bantu. Their game were being reduced by two causes. The Whites with their guns did not hesitate to enter their remaining hunting grounds and kill — often wastefully. Also there is no doubt that much of the larger game moved seasonally down from the cold uplands in the autumn when the grazing turned sour; and up again in the spring for the new green grass available there much earlier than on the plains below because of the higher early rainfall in the mountains. Some at least of the Bushmen hunters would have followed them. This they could no longer do and many of the animals would not come back, having been bagged by the White man, and by Bantu who also loved to hunt.

The Bushmen, naturally increasing in numbers while being more and restricted in territory with a decreasing food supply, has no alternative but to starve or hunt the domestic stock on the neighbouring farms and Bantu 'locations' which they considered their rightful hunting grounds anyway. They became expert rustlers, raiding at dawn

9

Plate 3

Steel's Shelter, Giant's Castle. Eland in polychrome and mounted hunters. For discussion see Section 3.

Plate 4

Steel's Shelter, Giant's Castle. Mounted hunter, and at bottom a child's copy. For description see Section 3.

10

Plate 5

Bushmen have stolen cattle and are driving them back into their mountain fastness. Pursuing farmers are about to be ambushed. The Bushmen have arrows in a band around their heads so that they can be quickly snatched and shot. One beast, failing to make the climb, is being stabbed to death to discourage the pursuers.

and driving off herds of cattle and horses back into mountains where they were slaughtered as required *(fig 5)*. There are several paintings of such scenes in the Underberg district. Sheep, of the fat tailed kind were also stolen *(fig 3)*. The farmers summoned their neighbours, formed a commando, and followed the spoor. Sometimes the raiders got away; sometimes they were overtaken, the men shot and

Fig. 5

The end of a cattle raid, men with spears close in for the kill. Bamboo hollow, Giants Castle.

the women and children taken to work on the farms. In 1869 a large scale onslaught was made upon them and the last large band destroyed. Minor raids continued until 1872 and the last known band, numbering a few, was seen in 1878 in what is now the Royal Natal National Park by a young couple on their ox-wagon honeymoon. Some remained in virtual captivity on the farms, and in parts of Lesotho over the border. The sad story of the extermination of the 'Berg Bushman has been told more fully in the works listed under 'Further Reading', in most detail by John Wright.

12

Plate 6
Mpongweni, Underberg District. Bushmen driving off stolen cattle and horses.

Plate 7

Ikanti Mountain, Sani Pass. Bushmen on trek apparently all males. At bottom figures sit around killed animals.

14

3. THE BUSHMAN WAY

Plate 8

Kalahari Bushmen and his wife next to their simple shelter. Note her large buttocks and incurved back.

The Bushmen were small people as we all know and as we can still see in the remnant of their race living in South-West Africa/Namibia and Botswana: the men averaging

15

about 142 cm (4'8") in height and the women being even smaller *(Plate 8)*. Both sexes had well developed buttocks but in the women much more so as here and on the thighs was conveniently stored much fat especially important when bearing and suckling children. The effect was increased by a marked inward curve of the back which also made the stomach protrude. In the paintings these traits are often clearly shown, and also the breasts, but in the males little attention was given to bodily form. However, the male organ, as you will see, was frequently shown. This, of course, was not for pornographic reasons, but was perfectly natural in people who, more often than not, went naked. The organ is shown as not pendulous but projecting horizontally. This is a Bushman characteristic, though shared by some Hottentots, and is called **penis rectus.** You will notice also that the organ is often shown with an attachment, most commonly like a bar across it. This is a problem feature which will be discussed later. The sexes in the paintings can usually be distinguished by the clothing; or by objects they carry; or by the activity depicted.

Men, when they wore anything, had a sort of loincloth formed by a triangular skin with one corner passed between the legs *(fig 6)*. This was worn tight to the body and is seldom visible in the paintings. By women a skin apron was worn 'fore and aft' *(fig 7)*. Both sexes, when the weather required it, wore a **kaross,** a skin cloak. This could be short like a cape, or medium length and made of a single skin of a smaller buck; or long reaching below the knees, made of a larger skin or several small ones sewn together. The larger karosses served also as blankets — the 'mattress' a thick bed of grass and certain plants, remains of which can still sometimes be found in the remoter caves. You might come across a painted figure waving a kaross — it was a Bushman method of signalling. Skins stretched out to dry and to be scraped and brayed with fat are depicted but not commonly. Skin caps were also worn, and sandals sometimes, by men and women.

The figures in the long karosses, which were worn only by mountain Bushmen (as well as Hottentots and Bantu), when seen in reproductions by persons with little knowledge of South African ethnography, evoked a theory that the people represented must be 'foreigners' who had travelled to South Africa in ancient times from Phoenicia or elsewhere in the Near East. The theory has long since been discredited. See my 1956 book under 'Further Reading'.

Body painting was practised as protection to the skin, as ornament, and as part of certain rituals.

Beads made from ostrich eggshell, or other shell, were worn strung as necklaces or as bands around the ankle, above the knee, or as a belt. Latterly glass beads were obtained from 'Bantu' who had got them from White traders.

Bushman equipment was limited and light — it had to be portable. Late in their history they learned from the Hottentots or 'Bantu' how to make small clay pots, otherwise they used as water containers ostrich eggshells, or the skins of small animals with the holes sewn up. These are sometimes identifiable in the paintings. Women had their digging sticks with or without the bored stone weight, and a leather bag, usually fringed, in which to carry the veld foods they gathered. They are also shown collecting firewood *(figs 8 & 10)*.

16

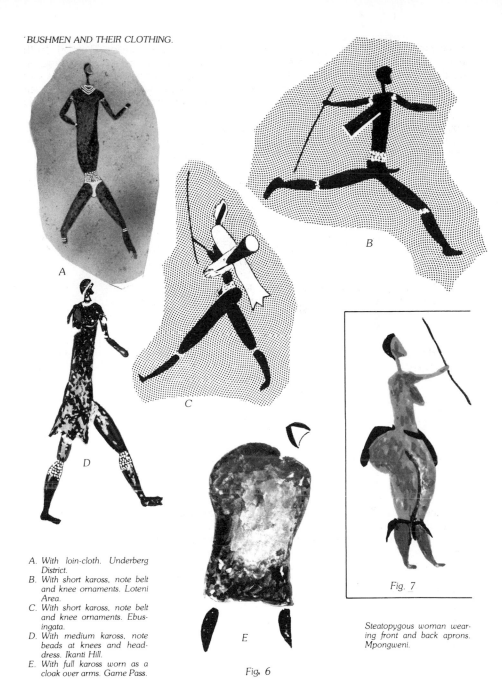

A. With loin-cloth. Underberg
   District.
B. With short kaross, note belt
   and knee ornaments. Loteni
   Area.
C. With short kaross, note belt
   and knee ornaments. Ebus-
   ingata.
D. With medium kaross, note
   beads at knees and headdress. Ikanti Hill.
E. With full kaross worn as a
   cloak over arms. Game Pass.

Fig. 6

Fig. 7

Steatopygous woman wear-
ing front and back aprons.
Mpongweni.

17

Plate 9

Ncibidwane Valley, Giant's Castle. Three figures with stylised heads wearing long karosses, and a bichrome eland.

We have good knowledge of the mens' equipment because of a lucky find by a farmer in one of the largest of the painted caves, the Eland Cave overlooking the Mhlwazini River valley between the Cathedral Peak and Cathkin Park resorts. On a high ledge he found a complete hunter's outfit placed there, no doubt, to be beyond reach of the children by the owner who never returned. The short 90cm (3′0) bow, strung with sinew, was contained in a hide case: in the 'Berg climate the bow-string had to be kept dry. There were 19 arrows, made from the thick coarse thatching grass and every light, tipped with bone or very small thin trinagular iron points, all well encrusted with poison. Below the poison is a small barb to keep the arrow in the wound while the venom did its work. The wooden spatula for applying it and a pouch containing one of the ingredients were part of the kit. There were two small metal knives, one with its rawhide sheath. The quiver was hollowed from some light wood and capped with hide. It had no carrying strap and was therefore probably carried in a

18

Fig. 8

A

B

A. Woman with weighted digging stick and collecting bag. Bulb also shown. Griqualand East.

B. Woman bringing in firewood, and child. Cathkin Area.

skin bag. Leather quivers with straps were also used and are commonly depicted and it is known from early traveller's accounts, and observable in the paintings, that when going into action the bowman would wear several arrows in a band around his head. From this they could be so quickly drawn that, according to one account, the archer could snatch and shoot ten arrows in as many seconds. The arrows around the head have sometimes been mistaken for hair standing on end *(fig 9 B)*.

They did sometimes use a wooden spear just sharpened or headed with bartered iron, probably to give a quick *coup de grace* to their kills. It was, moreover, a more effective weapon to use when hunting on horseback. Some horsemen are shown holding whips and a pronged stick which is probably a goad to urge on stolen stock *(fig 9 E)*. The men would also have their stone tools, fire sticks, and some of them their painting outfits. We would dearly like to find one of those but what is know of the artists' equipment will be stated later. Small knobbed sticks were carried to throw at birds such as quail that rose from the grass *(fig 9 C & D)*.

Figures carrying guns cannot for that reason alone be identified as Europeans. Bantu also acquired them by trade or as payment for services and Bushmen stole them whenever possible. Of course the depictions of guns can be used to date the paintings within the limits of about A.D. 1840-1880.

Another artefact was the tail of an animal such as a jackal fixed over the end of a small stick. This had all the uses of handkerchief and flywhisk. It was also used for gesticulating while dancing and for signalling *(fig 13A, figures on bridge)*.

A bushman hut was a very small and crudely built shelter made of sticks and grass or leaves, bee-hive shaped. They were hardly needed in cave country and are seldom depicted. When they are, it is sometimes in section to show the contents. Digging sticks were 'parked' outside *(fig 11)*.

19

A. Man with bow and quivers of arrows. Note body paint. Battle Cave.

B. Man with bow and arrows, some worn around head.
Eastern Lesotho.

C. Man with bow and knobbed stick. Note headdress. Underberg District.

D. Man with two knobbed throwing sticks. Underberg District.

E. Horseman with pronged goad. Mpongweni.

F. Dancer with rattle. Giant's Castle.

Fig. 9

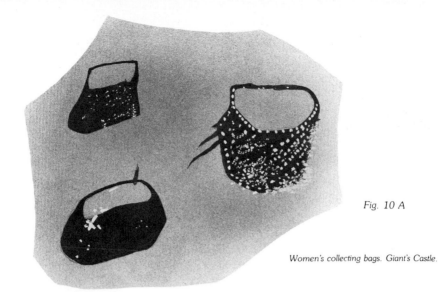

Fig. 10 A

Women's collecting bags. Giant's Castle.

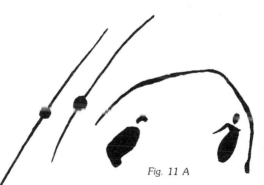

Fig. 10 B

Woman with bag as knapsack and weighted digging stick. Note wedge under the bored stone weight. Underberg District.

Fig. 11 A

Figures within hut or shelter and digging sticks outside. Ndhloveni Mountain.

Bushmen were very fond of honey. Property rights in the hives of the wild bees were recognised and jealously defended: honey was one of the few things Bushmen were prepared to fight over. Scenes of honey collecting have been recognised in the paintings and some groups of concentric curves *(fig 12 A)* are interpreted as showing honey-combs as made by rock bees. This is clear in some cases where they are

21

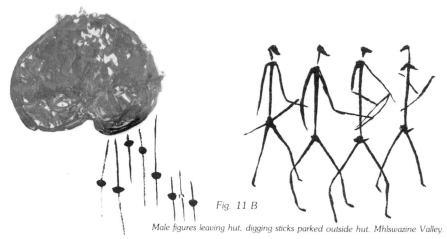

Fig. 11 B

Male figures leaving hut, digging sticks parked outside hut. Mhlswazine Valley.

accompanied by minute dots or even bichromes representing bees. More often the honey would be deep in crevices in the rock. Bee's nests can take various shapes some of which have also been identified in paintings. To reach the hives — usually high up in a rock face — ladders were made. This was done by driving wooden pegs into crevices to support rungs or by making rope ladders hung from a stake or tree at the top of a 'krans'. Remains of the pegs have been found in the 'Berg and paintings of the rope ladders are fairly common, especially in the Cathedral Peak area *(fig 12 B & C)*. Bushmen's ability to make ladders was known from travellers' accounts but that

Plate 10

The Eland Cave, Cathkin Area. At top figures sit next to small constructed shelters. Other figures run to the right and some shaded polychrome eland move to the left.

22

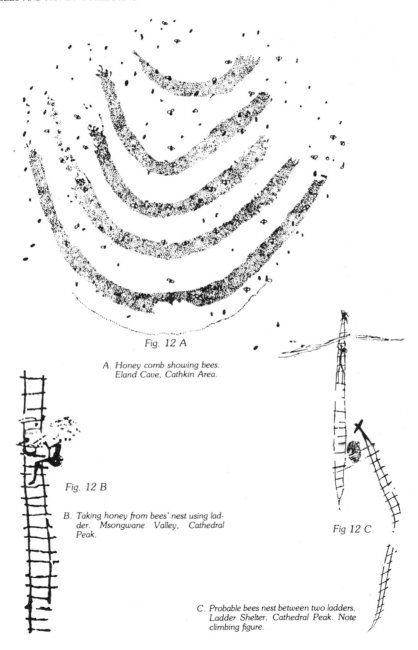

Fig. 12 A

A. Honey comb showing bees.
Eland Cave, Cathkin Area.

Fig. 12 B

B. Taking honey from bees' nest using ladder. Msongwane Valley, Cathedral Peak.

Fig 12 C

C. Probable bees nest between two ladders. Ladder Shelter, Cathedral Peak. Note climbing figure.

they made rope bridges is one of the facts learnt solely from the study of the rock paintings as two are quite clearly shown *(fig 13)*.

Also learnt from the paintings, but not recorded historically, is that they made small canoes or coracles, probably of sewn skins on a basket-like frame, from which to spear fish or angle for them *(fig 14)*. We did know that they had harpoons. They were seen in 1829 using them — long ones with poisoned points — to hunt hippos in the Umzimvubu River inland from Port St Johns.

The economic activities fo the Bushmen were vegetable food gathering (by women), hunting and fishing — and latterly stock raiding — by the men. These tasks took up but a small part of their time, leaving plenty of leisure for dancing, miming animal behaviour, story telling and painting. The other Bushmen art, **engraving** on the rocks, is not found in the Drakensberg.

Pictures of women with their digging sticks and skin collecting bags are fairly common *(figs 8 & 10)*.

BUSHMAN ROPE BRIDGES.

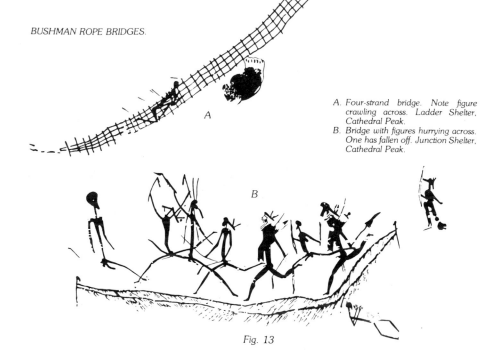

A. Four-strand bridge. Note figure crawling across. Ladder Shelter, Cathedral Peak.
B. Bridge with figures hurrying across. One has fallen off. Junction Shelter, Cathedral Peak.

A

B

Fig. 13

Hunting scenes can be recognised, knowing the methods used, and sometimes successful hunters are shown carrying a small buck slung over a shoulder *(Plate 11)*. Large kills such as eland were cut up and carried home in sections. Hunting methods included running down the animal until brought to a halt by exhaustion, driving the quarry into an ambush *(fig 15)*, and stalking. The latter method was helped by the hunter wearing the skin and head of an antelope or just the skin of the head as a cap *(fig 16)*. By slow approach, skillfully miming the animals actions and keeping well down in the grass, he could get close enough to loose his arrow. The animal disguises, however, do not always indicate hunting: they were also used when dancing *(Plate 12)*. Small animals were snared.

Fig. 14

Harpooning fish from
coracles. Mpongweni.
Underberg District.

A method still used by the Bushmen of the Kalahari to hunt burrow-living nocturnal animals such as the spring hare, antbear and porcupine, is by means of a long (up to 4 metres) thin and flexible stick with a barbed or hooked end. This is thrust into the burrow and with luck — for the hunter — into the animal which is then pulled, or dug out. There is a painting showing a man holding such a stick in the famous White Lady shelter in South-West Africa/Namibia and at least one, which will be later described, in the Drakensberg, where it could have been used to get ordinary hares, procupines, antbears and perhaps dassies.

Fig 15

Hunter driving eland
into ambush. Giant's
Castle.

25

Plate 11

Sebaaini Shelter, Ndedema Valley. Part of a long procession of hunters wearing animal disguise. The leading figure carries a killed buck.

Hunts of elephant are painted with the hunters surrounding and harrying the pachyderm and in some cases have been interpreted as showing the African method of running in and hamstringing the animal.

Another know Bushman method - the use of pitfalls — has not been recorded or found depicted in the 'Berg.

Sometimes the hunters became the hunted: there are several paintings showing them in full flight from a charging leopard. These scenes are painted with humour and apparently seen as something as a joke *(fig 17)*.

There were fish in the streams, at least below the higher waterfalls, and the method of spearing them, from floating craft or the bank, has ben mentioned. Delicate bone hooks, found in 'digs' show that they were anglers also. Conical basket traps used by Bushmen elsewhere in South Africa (and by Bantu) and shown in paintings in Lesotho have not been identified on the Natal side of the 'Berg, but is would be surprising if they were not used. Fish are rarely depicted in the northern part of the area but are fairly common towards Underberg.

26

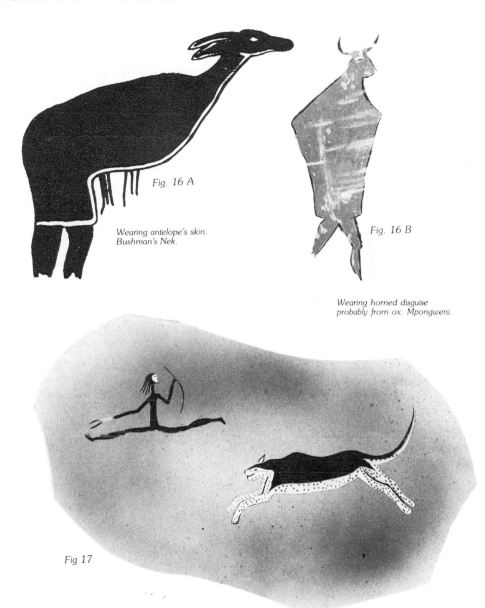

Fig. 16 A

Wearing antelope's skin.
Bushman's Nek.

Fig. 16 B

Wearing horned disguise
probably from ox. Mpongweni.

Fig 17

A hunter hunted. Man flees from leopard. Griqualand East.

Among the commonest scenes are dances *(figs 18 & 24).* From early records in other parts of South Africa and recent studies in the Kalahari we can recognise them and interpret the details. Women had their own dances connected with puberty and

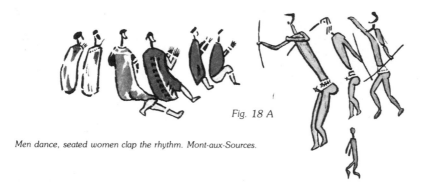

Fig. 18 A

Men dance, seated women clap the rhythm. Mont-aux-Sources.

other rituals, but men were the habitual dancers. Seldom did the sexes dance together: the womens' role was to sit by the fire and provide the music by singing, and the rhythm by clapping in unison. You will notice that they clapped with fingers apart: they still do. There are some paintings which show the men in confronting rows but generally the dancers moved in a circle taking shuffling or stamping steps and leaning forward somewhat. The dance was long continued and exhausting. It often caused bleeding from the nose. For many of the dancers it led to going into a state of trance,

Fig. 18 B

Dancer wearing skin mimes animal, seated women clap. Cathedral Peak.

falling to the ground and having to be revived. Just before entering trance the arms are thrown backwards and the dancer sinks to his knees, and it has been suggested that this was accompanied by the sensation of flying, so commonly reported by shamans and witches. While semi-conscious the man was believed to have powers of exorcism and healing. When unconscious his spirit was thought to leave the body and have super-natural experiences. Some of the paintings of creatures neither human nor animal might be attempts to depict what was remembered of such halucinations.

Giant's Castle Game Reserve. Winter view from Hutted Camp. The Main Caves are in the sandstone krans to right of centre. Nancy Willcox in foreground.

The Eland Cave, Cathkin Area. Alan Telford, Alex and Nancy Willcox outside the large painted shelter in the top band of sandstone. The basalt peaks Cathkin Peak, Champagne Castle and Sterkhorn in the background.

i

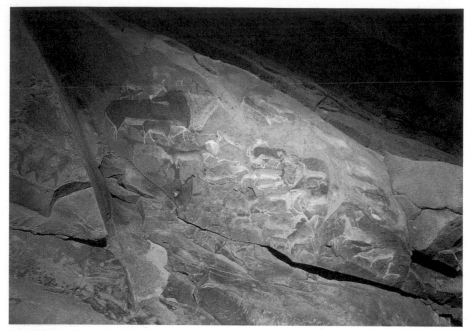

The Eland Cave, Cathkin Area. The main panel of paintings. Mainly of eland but with human figures and roan antelope also. For further description see Section 3.

Kamberg Nature Reserve. A bull eland — the Bushman's delight — one of a herd kept in fenced area under observation as an experiment in domestication.

Battle Cave, Giant's Castle Game Reserve. The battle scene. For full description see Section 3 and for details Plates 14 & 15.

Sorcerer's Shelter, Ndedema Gorge. Mythical creature on left as shown in fig 20F, meandering lines, two fine rhebuck and faintly on right a blue crane.

Xeni Stream, Cathedral Peak Area. Rhebuck, a bushbuck and a group of Bushmen on left, on right a foreshortened rear view of a buck. For full description see Section 3.

Main Cave, Giant's Castle Game Reserve. On left a cloaked figure, at centre two masked hunters, at top left a feline. For full description see Section 3.

Willcox's Shelter,
Giant's Castle Game
Reserve. The mythical
creature called the
'Moon Godess'. See
also fig. 20G and for
full description
Section 3.

Game Pass Shelter, Kamberg Area. The main panel of paintings. Eland, cloaked figures and tiny running figures forming three or four layers of paintings. For full description see Section 3. The Willcox children Sandra and David below had an early introduction to Bushman art.

Sandra's Shelter, Kamberg Area. Miniature masterpiece of a howling black-backed jackal. The scale shown is 3 inches. See Section 3 for further description.

Nuttall's Shelter, Kamberg Area. One of rather rare paintings of the common reedbuck. Note forward sweep of horns.

Ulonyama, Kamberg Area. Dancers in a circle. The indistinct figure in the centre is probably a dancer in the trance state being revived.

Mpongweni, Underberg District. A group of dancers with women on both sides clapping the rhythm. For further description see Section 3.

Nuttall's Shelter, Kamberg Area. A pig hunt that went wrong. The pig is chasing some of the hunters.

The Meads, Griqualand East. The panel of paintings, all of eland, has been cut out and is now displayed in the Natal Museum, Pietermaritzburg. Note the foreshortened rear view on the left, the modelling of the animal in profile next to it and the one on the right shown as lying down and seen from above.

The circular movement of the dancers left a track in the ground which is shown in at least one painting.

Plate 12

Tabamyama, Giant's Castle. Four males dance in a circle around another wearing an antelope head mask. A similar figure stands around the corner of the rock. Note the perspective.

Although dancing was usually a group activity, of great social importance, it is clear from the paintings that a dancer would execute a *pas seul*, in some cases wearing an animal's skin or head mask, and no doubt miming the animal's actions. Such figures may be shown crouching and holding a stick in each hand as part of the front legs of the animal *(Colour Plates XIII and XIV)*.

We do not know whether the 'Berg Bushmen used any musical instruments. Probably they did as elsewhere they are known to have used the hunting bow or adaptations of it, and a simple drum, to make music: and dancers wore rattles made of seed filled cocoons tied to their ankles. These instruments have not yet been identified with any certainty in the paintings, but should be looked for. I would myself interpret some of the small club-like objects carried by dancing figures as rattles *(fig 9 F)*.

In the rather uncommon scenes of fighting between bands of Bushmen there is much animation and detail. Arrows fly through the air, men run into the fray, or walk out of it wounded *(Colour Plate V)*. Casualties lie bleeding *(fig 15)*. The bow was the

29

Plate 13

Mpongweni, Underberg District. A baboon-like creature with a bent tail performs in the centre while others dance around. For full description see Section 3.

usual weapon with hardly any representations of hand-to-hand combat but a few paintings show a knobkerry or a weighted digging stick being used as a club *(Plate 21)*.

Many skirmishes took place between Bushmen cattle raiders and the pursuing Bantu or European owners of the stolen beasts *(Plate 5)*. An extraordinarily detailed scene of a commando catching up with Bushmen raiders can be seen near Underberg.

A few paintings have been interpreted as burial scenes and we must presume that the Bushmen did bury their dead here as they did elsewhere. But so far no Bushmen interrements have been discovered in the 'Berg; all that have been found were of Bantu with some Bushman admixture.

That the Bushmen had a rich mythology is well known from voluminous records made in the Cape and, more recently, from the Kalahari tribes. Some stories and beliefs were also noted on the Lesotho side of the escarpment. How much was shared by the Natal Bushmen is not known. It is extraordinary that there is not one account by an anthropologist, traveller or missionary, of visiting them at their habitations to study their folklore and way of life: and to ask the questions regarding the interpretation of the paintings and the motives of the artists, to which we must now seek answers elsewhere. Hostility between the two races no doubt prevented this, but there were many 'tame' or captive Bushmen on the farms for two generations from whom much could have been learnt. There can, however, be no doubt that some of the strange creatures depicted illustrate folk tales or represent supernatural beings they believed in.

30

Plate 14

Battle Cave, Giant's Castle. A detail of the battle scene — see Colour Plate V and full description in Section 3. Women on left restrain their males. Other men rush into the fray.

The principal figure in the mythology of the Bushmen of the Western Cape was a being called Kaggen who, while not being quite a deity, had all sorts of supernatural powers. The beliefs connected with him were to some extent shared by Bushmen of western Lesotho. He most commonly manifested himself as the praying mantis *(Mantis religiosa)*, which curious insect was also revered by the Hottentots, but he could take other forms at will and appear, for example, as a hartebeest, a hare, or

31

Plate 15

Battle Cave, Giant's Castle. A detail of the battle scene. An elaborately painted figure runs to the left. A casualty bleeding from the arm walks out and another bleeding from the arm and head lies *hors de combat.*

even a louse. He created the eland in which he maintained a special interest. His interventions in the Bushmen's world were sometimes beneficent, sometimes mischievious. It is somewhat surprising, therefore, that no clear representations are known in the paintings of the Mantis **as such** although of course he might be in others of his manifestations. Perhaps the figure illustrated which looks half man and half mantis is Kaggen *(fig 19)*. 'Mantis' incidentally is the latinised form of Greek word for the insect meaning 'diviner', as the Greeks also attributed supernatural powers to it, including the gift of prophecy.

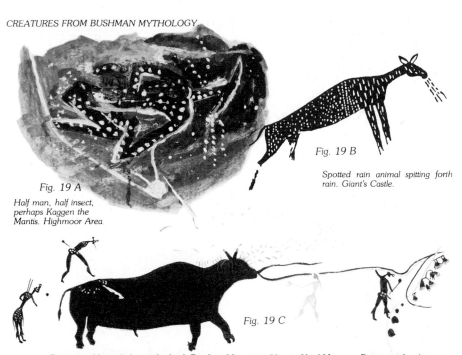

Fig. 19 A

Half man, half insect,
perhaps Kaggen the
Mantis. Highmoor Area.

Fig. 19 B

Spotted rain animal spitting forth
rain. Giant's Castle.

Fig. 19 C

Rain animal being led over the land. Bamboo Mountain. (Now in Natal Museum, Pietermaritzburg).

Plate 16

Battle Cave, Giant's Castle. Three insect-like figures on left face an animal headed dancer or medicine man superimposed on an eland. See also Section 3.

33

Recorded Bushman lore is full of stories of humans taking the form of animals or vice versa. Clearly they had a feeling of kinship with the animals about them, indeed a kind of empathy. Cape Bushmen told scholar W.H.I. Bleek that they could "feel" in their own feet the feet of the springbok as it came, feel in their eyes the black marks on the animals's eyes, and feel on their faces the black stripes on its face. This feeling may explain many of the paintings which show creatures part animal, part human, and are referred to as *therianthropes (Plate 17)*. These should not be confused with people dressed up for hunting, dancing or ritual purposes. Sometimes, you will notice figures shown with hooves, but human in other respects.

The Cape Bushmen told of a rain-bull or rain-animal said to live in a pool. Their rain doctors claimed that when rain was needed, they located it, lassood it, and led the creature over the land. Wherever it trod rain fell. This was a personification, or rather an animalisation, of the rain cloud which bellowed i.e. thundered: and whose legs were descending columns of rain. The animal is depicted sometimes like an eland,

Plate 17

Mushroom Hill, Cathedral Peak Area. 'Therianthropes', part animal and part human, holding unidentified objects. For full description see Section 3.

34

sometimes more like a hippo, is sometime spotted, and sometimes is shown under a rainbow. Although there are instances of spotted animals in the 'Berg paintings obviously not leopards or other cats *(fig 19 B)*, depictions of mythical rain animals are doubtful except for one example removed to Durban Museum *(fig 19 C)*. In this high rainfall area rain-making was probably not such an important preoccupation as it was elsewhere.

Another widespread myth, believed also by Bantu, was of a great snake, python-like but with an animal's head or horns *(fig 20 A)*.

CREATURES FROM BUSHMAN MYTHOLOGY.

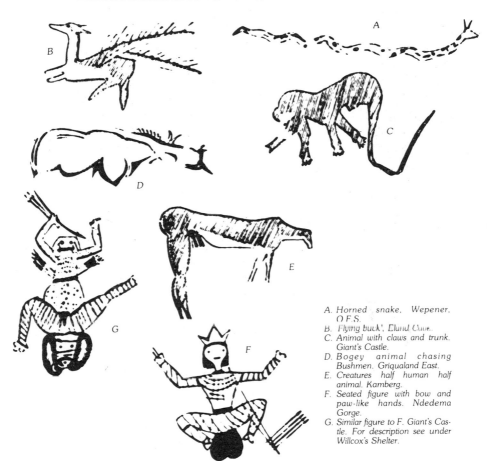

A. Horned snake. Wepener, O.F.S.
B. Flying buck', Eland Cave.
C. Animal with claws and trunk. Giant's Castle.
D. Bogey animal chasing Bushmen. Griqualand East.
E. Creatures half human half animal. Kamberg.
F. Seated figure with bow and paw-like hands. Ndedema Gorge.
G. Similar figure to F. Giant's Castle. For description see under Willcox's Shelter.

Fig. 20

35

Other odd paintings, quite common in the 'Berg, are of creatures with wings or wing-like appendages, though seemingly not birds, bats or insects *(figs 20 B & 21)*. The first to be noted looked liked antelope and were described as 'flying buck' but they exist in great variety. Some have human legs and the 'wings' look more like arms thrown back, others are more like animals or birds. The 'arms back' position, it has been pointed out, is the attitude of a dancer before going into a trance and it has been suggested that these figures illustrate how the artist remembered feeling, or seeing himself by hallucination, at that moment. Other theories are that they symbolised the spirit or soul of a Bushman, temporarily or permanently out of the body, or in some cases that of an animal at death. They have also been described (by Patricia Vinnicombe — see 'Further Reading') as 'intermediaries between earth and sky'. For the trance theory above mentioned see Lewis-Williams' book listed. But what do you think?

There are a few 'bogey animals' shown with gaping jaws chasing people *(fig 20 B)*.

Some imaginary creatures may be based on myth or be the personal flight of fancy of the artist. If repeated over a wide area it is of course more likely to be the former. The ones shown *(fig 20 F & G)* are sufficently alike to represent the same conception and are about 40 km (25 miles) apart *(Colour Plates VI & IX)*. There is a similar one in Lesotho so this figure is more probably from the mythology of the 'Berg Bushmen of which, as I have sadly remarked, virtually nothing is known.

CREATURES FROM BUSHMAN MYTHOLOGY.

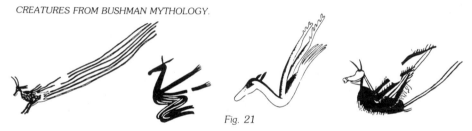

Fig. 21

Examples of the mysterious winged figures. Various sites.

Who were the artists: what was their sex and status? There can be no certainty, but all those reported to have been seen at work, or to have had painting equipment, were men. From the standard of the work it seems certain that they were trained people and that not everybody painted, at least in the home shelter. There is evidence that some of them had a special faculty of what might be called mental photography and vivid recall. It might be that they combined the roles of artist and medicine men, as was the case with the American Indian shamans, and that some of the paintings were executed as part of a ritual. This however, would explain but a small part of the subject matter of the art!

The Bushman 'band' would consist of a basic three-generation family with perhaps a few hangers-on also related, amounting to about 20 to 30 persons including the children. In the case of the Kalahari Bushmen the average number is about 30. It is conjectural, but likely, that in seasons of plenty they would come together in larger numbers at one of the big caves for purely social reasons — family reunions, the meeting of young people as potential mates, dancing, story-telling and other pleasurable activities: but would then separate again into the family units which could feed themselves without having to range over too large an area to gather veld foods.

4.   THE ANIMALS OF THE 'BERG AND THE PAINTINGS

All the large animals still in the area shown in the paintings. Some are depicted which are no longer there and consideration of these cases has led to the reintroduction of some species as having a good chance of success. It is one of the mysteries of the art that some small animals, among the commonest and known to have been a source of food for the Bushmen, are not depicted or very rarely. Examples are the dassie (hyrax or rock-rabbit), the hare, the mongoose and similar animals, and the small rodents. I know of only one rat. This selectivity might be a clue to the purpose of the art: the question will be discussed later.

Plate 18
Willem's Shelter, Kamberg Area. Galloping hartebeeste. The speed of this very fleet animal is indicated by painting the legs more faintly than the body.

Animals reintroduced are the black wildebeeste, distinguished from the blue wildebeeste by the horns curving downwards **and forwards** and up again; and the Cape (or red) hartebeest. There are only half a dozen recorded representations of the black wildebeeste; hartebeest are fairly common. There are a good many roan antelope paintings and reintroduction of these animals might be considered. Also recently reintroduced is the blesbok, very easily identified by the white blaze (bless in Afrikaans) on its face, and lyreshaped horns. Although stated in some books to be a **reintroduction** I can find no historical evidence that it was ever present in the 'Berg; and among the thousands of antelope in the paintings I know of no certain representation of it.

Only one painting of a zebra, or the related quagga, is on record. Its virtual absence and the rarity of the black wildebeeste in the paintings is understandable — both are animals of the plains. The true mountain zebra of the Cape did not range so far.

From the evidence of the paintings, elephants came up the valleys, probably only seasonally, and were hunted, latterly for their tusks as well as for their meat. Historically it is known that the ivory was bartered to the Bantu and eventually much of it reached the White traders.

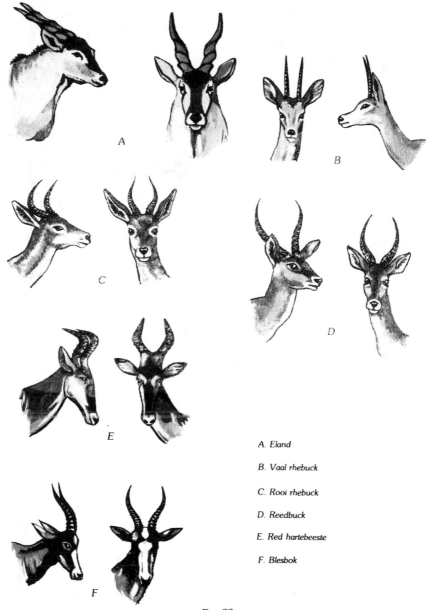

A. Eland

B. Vaal rhebuck

C. Rooi rhebuck

D. Reedbuck

E. Red hartebeeste

F. Blesbok

Fig. 22

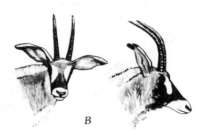

B

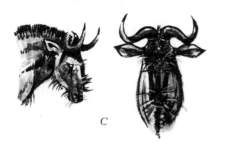

C

D

E

A. Bushbuck

B. Roan antelope

C. Black wildebeest

D. Oribi

E. Grey duiker

F. Klipspringer

F

Fig. 23

39

Plate 19

Battle Cave, Giant's Castle. A cat, presumably a leopard 'though not spotted, painted over human figures.

A few leopards still exist in the 'Berg but you are very unlikely to see one of these wary beasts, except in the paintings as already mentioned *(Plate 19)*. Other cats, the serval, and the caracal or lynx, are occasionally seen and might be among the felines depicted but not clearly identifiable. There are a few paintings of lions which no doubt sometimes followed the buck on their springtime return to the mountain pastures.

Hyenas have been recognised in the paintings but not seen, the black-backed jackal can be encountered in the flesh and in paint *(Plate XI))*.

Paintings of the still abundant baboons are common, but I know of no monkeys, although the vervet monkey frequents the patches of forests.

Other animals existing but very rarely seen are porcupines - I know of no paintings of them — antbears of which there are a few representations, and bushpigs, of which there are also a few paintings *(Plates 20 & 21)*. Warthogs have not been reported in the 'Berg or in the paintings.

Not present now in the 'Berg, and probably never there, were the Cape buffalo and the rhinoceros. I know of only one painting of each of them.

Snakes are uncommon as painting subjects and are usually unidentifiable as to species, or obviously mythical. Two at Giant's Castle look like pythons *(Plate 22)*. The only large snakes possibly to be encountered within the Little 'Berg are the ringhals and the puff-adder, but the python might linger yet. I have heard stories of its being seen, and there have been reports of seeing the Cape cobra. The small 'Berg adder might also be seen or varieties of small and harmless snakes.

The occurrence of paintings of fish has been mentioned above. Insects? There are one or two possibles apart from bees shown as dots about their hives. The latter are formed of several superimposed layers of comb *(fig 12A)*. These paintings have so far been found only in the northern part of our area.

Domestic animals include numerous cattle and horses, a few sheep, perhaps a goat or two, and dogs, the only animal kept by the Bushmen themselves.

40

Plate 20
Battle Cave, Giant's Castle. Thought to be rhinos by some but I think bushpigs.

Plate 21
Bushpig Shelter, Giant's Castle. Good pig at top left. At right a fight in which one combatant uses a weighted digging stick as a club.

41

Plate 22

Main Cave (Western) Giant's Castle. A snake in polychrome, probably a python, and human figures.

The antelope now present are those mentioned above, also the eland, the grey rhebuck (Afrikaans vaalribbok), mountain reedbuck (rooiribbok), oribi, klipspringer, bushbuck and grey duiker, and possibly the grysbok (once common): the ones you are most likely to see being the first three named. The common reedbuck has also been reported but judging by its infrequency in the art (I know only of three clear cases) it was uncommon and is no longer present except in a few vleis in the valleys *(Colour plate XII)*.

Their recognition in the paintings presents problems only with regard to the smaller buck. The eland is usually painted with careful attention to such details as the light coloured parts of the body, the large withers and dewlap, the crease or roll of fat on the neck, the slight twist of the horns, and the dark hooves and tuft on the long tail. The black wildebeeste is unmistakable and so is the red hartebeeste with its long horse-like nose, marked withers and backward slope of the body. The heart shaped light patch (Afrikaans *hart*), on the rump is also shown. The horns which both sexes have, are quite distinctive bending sharply backwards. The tail is dark.

The bushbuck may sometimes be recognised by a dark 'collar' and a white band below it; and by the corkscrew twist of the horns (present in the male only) which slope backwards.

With other small antelope the difficulties are that they are usually painted to a small scale and the fact that the artists seldom bothered to match with their paint the actual colour of the object. They did, however, usually differentiate between the lighter and

42

Plate 23

Mpongweni, Underberg District. Polychrome eland and human figures with child's copy at bottom left. See Section 3 for full description.

darker parts of the body. Distinguishing between them, even in the flesh, is made more difficult because there can be variations in colour and body markings in the same species, and you may not be seeing the mature animal with its adult colour and developed horns. The horns if shown can be decisive but they occur only on the males in the case of the grey rhebok, mountain reedbuck, common reedbuck and (usually) the grey duiker.

The grey rhebok has almost straight medium length horns and bigger ears than the mountain reedbuck which like the common reedbuck, has horns curving forward. The oribi has short straight horns, so has the grey duiker but even shorter. Tails may help: in the reedbucks and the grey rhebuck the underside of the tail is white and is 'flashed' as a warning signal. It is shorter in the rhebok. The oribi has a black tail.

43

Plate 24

Game Pass Shelter, Kamberg Area. Polychrome eland with head turned forward and human figures. For discussion see Section 3.

Plate 25

Knuffel's Shelter, also called Rhebok Shelter, Cathedral Peak. Herd of vaal rhebok in mating season, playing and courting. Note mating couple at top left.

Plate 26
Baboon Cave, The Cavern, Mount-aux-Sources Area. Miniature paintings (about 5cm long) of a grey rhebok and a reclining doe beautifully 'modelled'.

Plate 27
Ikanti Mountain, Sani Pass. Very delicately painted grey rhebuck. Below to the right are rows of finger dots, perhaps a tally of buck killed.

The klipspringer also has very straight horns but may be distinguished by its chunkier body and being shown with its legs well under the body.

Paintings of the roan antelope, no longer present, are easily recognised by the backward curve of the long horns, shared (and exceeded) only by the sable antelope which there is no reason to believe was ever present. Its white muzzle with a dark patch above it is sometimes clearly shown.

About forty per cent of the 'Berg rock paintings are of animals, and of these nearly seventy per cent are of antelope. More than half of the antelope paintings are of eland. This is out of all proportion to the actual antelope population: eland can never have been very numerous as they require a great deal of living space. Certainly they were greatly outnumbered by the smaller buck taken together. So this over-representation requires explanation and again may yield a clue to the motives of the artists which will be discussed later.

5. THE PAINTERS' MATERIALS AND TECHNIQUES

Since no painting in the 'Berg is less than about a century old and all are exposed to considerable changes in atmospheric temperature and humidity, the clarity of many of them is remarkable. In a few cases they are fully exposed both to rain and sunshine and are at least still visible. Clearly the Bushmen were no mean paint technologists. Analysis and traditions indicate that they drew their material from many sources.

The pigments were chiefly mineral oxides, the different oxides of iron providing the various shades of red, brown and yellow which were the commonest colours used. The range of colours could be increased by 'burning' at the fire. Black was from charcoal or carbon from burnt bone, and possibly from manganese; white was from zinc oxide, clay, powdered quartz, or bird droppings. You may notice in the sandstone more or less spherical nodules and you may see places where they have been cut out. If broken open many are seen to contain powder. According to tradition in the Cape this was used to make paint and the broken nodules were called 'Bushman paintpots'. This has been confirmed by finding some with colour in them and by laboratory experiments in which the powder was subjected to varying degrees of heat and produced colours ranging over a wide spectrum from yellow to red, brown and black. Vermilion or a colour very near to it in the chromatic scale is sometimes — but very rarely — to be seen. The source of vermilion is by definition cinnabar (sulphide of mercury). Whether the Bushmen found and used this or another source of this brilliant red we do not know. A report early in this century that cinnabar had been found in the Drakensberg caused something of a prospectors 'rush' but it was not confirmed.

The solid pigments had to be ground to powder and I found upper and lower grindstones with colour on them in a 'dig' at Giant's Castle. Then of course, they had to be mixed with a liquid or semi-liquid medium to make paint. Again according to indirect information — apparently no one ever asked a Bushman how he made his paint — this was most often fat or certain plant saps, but egg and blood have also been mentioned and experiments have shown that they do produce good paint. The use of blood has been confirmed by recent analyses.

To contain the paint the horns of small antelope were used as well as the 'Bushman paintpots'. A Bushman shot in the Cape had ten of them hanging from his belt, each containing paint of a different colour.

Although feathers are reported to have been used to apply the paint, the fine work could have been done only with a brush and this is confirmed by two independent witnesses (both Bantu) who claimed to have watched Bushmen artists at work. The brush was made from hairs of the tail or mane of the black wildebeeste tied to the end of a thin reed. Later the hair from a horse was found to serve. One account, from a white farmer who also claimed to be an eye witness, states that they used pointed pieces of bone dipped in the viscous paint for drawing outlines and putting in fine details.

As we shall note in the next chapter paintings are in one, two, or more than two colours — referred to as monochromes, bichromes and polychromes respectively. In the monochromes a drawn outline is seldom observable but in the polychromes it is fairly common. A difficulty in applying colour to a surface arises where absorption may be uneven and show varying intensity of colour in the result. This is why modern artists prime their canvases or wall surfaces. A study of uncompleted Bushmen's

47

paintings, and ones from which a flake of the final colour is missing, shows that their artists did the same, first applying white paint over the whole area of the painting.

The second colour was then put on, in the case of bichrome and polychormes leaving the white visible where desired. Sometimes you may observe where the priming goes somewhat beyond the subsequent paint; sometimes this was clearly done to form an outline.

In the bichromes and polychromes of animals the artist most often made a sharp division between the colours even where this was not so in Nature, but in a late development merged the one gradually into the other — often with great delicacy — to produce the 'shaded polychromes'. This technique was used chiefly in painting of eland to achieve better agreement with the natural colouring, rather less often with other buck such as rhebuck, rarely on other animals, hardly ever on cattle paintings.

A remarkable point of technique in a few animal paintings where they are shown in the lateral aspect is leaving a slight gap between the two 'off' legs and the body, to show that they are the legs on the further side and avoid a confused picture. This I have called the 'Lascaux technique' as it was practised there and perhaps elsewhere in the cave art of Europe as well as by the Bushmen of South Africa — and as far as I know by no other prehistoric artists.

We do not know whether the artist made a preliminary sketch on a piece of stone or other material before starting work on the rock. One hearsay account from Lesotho says they did, but none has ever been found in the many archaeological excavations made in the painted shelters. Painted stones have been found in cave deposits in the Cape, usually interred with human remains and known as grave stones. They were not apparently used as sketches for wall paintings and they have not been found in 'digs' elsewhere.

6. THE PAINTINGS AS ART

The Bushman art of Southern Africa has been described by some writers, with no real knowledge of it, as 'primitive' or even 'childlike'. It is neither! It lacks truly primitive characteristics and indeed exhibits some sophistication. It avoids the limitations of childrens' art both in skill and degree of naturalism.

In primitive art, even in the early art of civilised peoples — of Egypt, the Near East, even Greece — paintings of animals soon became stereotyped, herds of them were painted all very much alike and shown proceeding in a row one behind the other; and all in profile. Men also, even in battle, are shown as alike as lead soldiers, in orderly arrangements and in set attitudes, one side to the left, the other to the right. In Bushman art every animal in a herd (say of eland) will be seen to differ from the others in detail, proportion or action; the herd is shown often in depth and the animals in many aspects, not merely lateral profile. And the primitive characteristic of painting only the two near legs of a quadruped is very rare, at least in the Drakensberg. Moreover, a Bushman battle scene is shown as the melee it was, men running into the fray loosing arrows, or fleeing, turning to stand again, in all kinds of attitudes.

The art on the rocks is superior to what is generally called children's art not only technically in its sensitive drawing and skilful application of paint, but also by being perceptual — based upon what is seen and recalled — not distorted by knowledge and concept as children's art is, except in special cases. Children tend to paint what they know to be there, whether they can see it or not, and according to the strength of concepts in the child's mind. In the paintings of animals details such as the eye, horns and tail, are usually exaggerated. The Bushman artist, on the other hand, painted animals as he saw them, subordinating detail to the whole. His painting is a visual image recreated, 'though he might slightly stress characteristics such as the length of an eland or the bulk of an elephant. These remarks apply to the paintings of animals only — that they are painted naturalistically — not to the Bushmen's paintings of human figures which are stylised. This distinction you may observe in any painted shelter where you will note that the human figures are never painted with anything like the fidelity to actual form as are the animals. Observe the heads — almost always featureless, often mere blobs. The part of the head covered with hair might be given a different colour from the face. That is all, there is nothing like a portrait. The differing modes of painting animals and humans pose another question to be discussed later with the 'problems'. You will notice, however, that women are sometimes shown with somewhat greater naturalism — the body, not the head — and this may perhaps be expected if the artists were male.

Note also that the human figures seldom appear singly; they occur in groups, almost always in some kind of individual action or group activity such as dancing or 'trekking', whereas animals, though also often shown in groups, are commonly shown singly and may be in quite static attitudes.

Let us examine the art in detail. About sixty per cent of the figures are in one colour — monochromes — red being the favourite colour followed by black and white equally, then orange, yellow, brown, grey and vermilion. Studies have shown that the use of black, yellow, orange and vermilion is commoner in the later paintings with a decrease in use of the dark red. This probably resulted from the late discovery of new pigment sources. The choice did not depend on the actual colour of the object, an elephant for example is more likely to be painted in red than grey. About twenty per cent are in two colours — bichromes — and the rest polychromes with or without shading.

Size varies from minute — a dot representing a bee which even so may be in two colours — to more than two metres (6ft) in some paintings of eland. There is no kind of consistancy of scale: this depended on the artist's preference or the size of the 'canvas'. Thus elephants are painted no bigger than the eland. Eland paintings, however, are on the average larger than rhebuck. Where animals and men occur together in the same scene, the relative sizes are usually about right.

The art is as remarkable for what is not depicted as for what is. Scenery is virtually absent: there are only two or three known attempts in the whole 'Berg area. Very rarely a ground line is painted along which animal or human figures move: and there are some lines which are apparently tracks. Plants are equally rare as painting subjects in spite of their importance in Bushman diet, and as sources of paint and poison ingredients. The extreme rarity of the smaller food animals has already been noted.

Absent also in the 'Berg paintings are the geometrical forms such as spirals, divided and concentric circles, grid patterns, et cetera, and the amorphous designs, found in Bushman art in other regions and almost universally in prehistoric rock art elsewhere: in that of Australia and North America for example. All the 'Berg art is figurative, representations of animals, humans, mythical beings and objects, although a few of the latter are not certainly identified. An element strangely absent is handprints, also almost universal in rock art and found in the Cape, Transvaal, S.W. Africa/Namibia and Zimbabwe. I would be glad to hear of any examples discovered.

Another surprise is the avoidance of sexual themes other than indicating the sex of the human figures. Two or three paintings of humans have been identified as copulation or rape scenes. Even these are doubtful! Some of the antelope paintings show the animals engaged in courting and pre-mating behaviour. Only one clear case of animal mating is known — a rhebock ram mounting a doe *(Plate 25)*.

Perhaps the most remarkable characteristic of Bushman art is the ability to paint animals in foreshortened attitudes as seen from the front or the rear *(Colour Plate XVI)*, or — even more difficult — in three-quarter view. This is not found in prehistoric rock art anywhere else in the world, and the painters of medieval Europe were slow to learn it.

Other difficult attitudes are those showing the animal lying down with the head turned back, and standing 'sideways on' with the head turned to the front.

Some artists achieved perspective, as in the dance and the file of horses illustrated *(fig. 24)*.

Depth was given to scenes or groups by painting them as if looked down upon from a slightly higher viewpoint.

Action was skilfully depicted especially in the human figures and it is noticeable that the figure is usually simplified in these cases, as it is the action not the form which it was desired to depict. This is true to a lesser degree of the animal paintings. In the human figures shown running the leg action may be deliberately exaggerated so that the legs are in a straight line: this is deliberate emphasis. An extraordinary expressiveness was achieved in scenes involving two or more persons. For example see fig 25. At A the woman on the left might be saying 'let me hold the baby' and the one at B 'don't get involved in the fight dear'.

Some may consider the miniatures to be the finest examples of painting skill. They are most commonly pictures of rhebok or other small antelope, sometimes less than 8 cm (3 inches) overall but executed in bichrome or polychrome and in all possible

Fig. 24 A

Circular dance around central figure. Giant's Castle

Fig. 24 B

File of horsemen. Giant's Castle.

attitudes. Even the legs — of less than matchstick thickness — may be in two colours *(Plates 26 & 27, plate VI).*

It will be observed that some paintings have been superimposed upon others. In fact four or five 'layers' of paintings can sometimes be made out. This shows the relative ages of the paintings involved but not the time interval between them. You will, however, often see polychromes especially the shaded ones painted over other

51

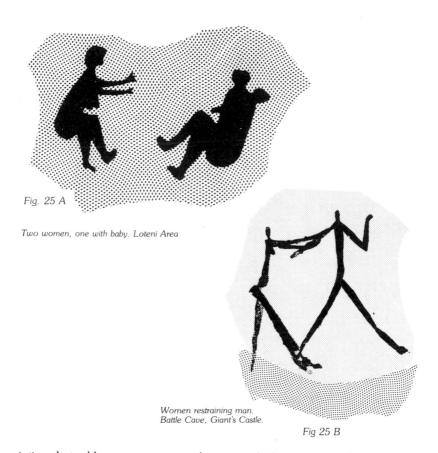

Fig. 25 A

Two women, one with baby. Loteni Area

Women restraining man.
Battle Cave, Giant's Castle.

Fig 25 B

paintings but seldom see any monochromes or bichromes painted over polychromes. From this and their apparent freshness and the fact that the shaded polychromes are found within the area to which the Bushmen were restricted only a few centuries ago, we know that they were a late development. This did not mean that the older kinds of paintings were no longer made, at least by some artists, and it is clear that the monochrome (usually red) human figures were painted from the earliest times until the end.

A feature strange to the eye of those unaquainted with prehistoric rock art, whether that of Europe, Africa or elsewhere, and accustomed to seeing mural art and framed pictures, is the absence of 'background' in the rock art. There is no attempt to fill in with paint between the figures, or around them within a real or imaginary frame, or to put in irrelevant detail. The effect is to concentrate attention on the figures.

52

7. A BUSHMAN CAVE

Come with me in imagination to a painted shelter and learn how to look at the art. Not an actual one, but a composite of several in order to exhibit a good variety of paintings. Let us not be in a hurry! Ideally we should sleep with the paintings, where this is permitted; see them in the evening and morning light, gain empathy with the artists, look out and quite likely see some of the animals they saw.

I shall advise you to start your study of the paintings by standing back to observe the general arrangement, then make a first survey. Note carefully the relative ages of the paintings as shown by the order of superpositioning — what is painted upon what. This helps to determine which paintings were done at the same time, and which therefore may be part of a scene. For example, is that man with the arrow notched to his bowstring really shooting at that animal, or do the man and the animal belong to a different period? Mistakes about this, what is called 'false grouping', can lead to surprising interpretations. People can be on apparently intimate terms with wild animals or appear to be jumping over them. A well-known painting in the Cape appeared to show a man feeding an eland and it was taken to show that the Bushman had domesticated the animal (which might have happened!), until it was realised that the man, with other similar figures, belonged to an older series of paintings than the eland.

Try to put yourself in the position of the first artist at the shelter looking at the virgin rock face. Where would he choose to start? As there is every evidence that the painters wanted their work to last, it was presumably a well protected position which is usually near the centre in the case of a small shelter. Also, no doubt, he would want a good expanse of reasonably smooth and not discoloured rock, preferably easy to reach and, assuming that they were like other artists, where his work could be seen and admired. When these requirements or some of them were to be found you might expect to find the oldest paintings. See if this is true. If it appears to be, what is the painting, the subject and technique?

You have established the order in time and the groupings as far as you can. Identify the animals: if any domestic kinds are shown this will help to confirm the relative ages of the paintings (Section 1:2). If for example anything is painted over a horse it is very late. Determine the sex of the human figures, where possible, note the equipment and the activity depicted. Now you can read the scenes — dances, hunts, fights, parties on trek with their few possessions, a cattle raid, perhaps a scene illustrating a myth or dreamed up by the artist.

You may be interested to look at the male figures to note the attachment to the penis mentioned in Section 1:3, and ponder its meaning.

Observe whether the kinds of paintings tend to be at different heights above the cave floor: this can be significant. Look especially at the lower 1 metre (3 feet) of the rock face. Here you might find childrens' art, recognisable by being less skilfully executed and usually an attempt to imitate an adult painting higher up. Could some of the high up paintings have been made only from a ladder or scaffold?

You might find it of interest to count the figures engaged in the dances or domestic scenes and compare the result with the probable numbers of actual occupants of the shelter. For practical reasons it is thought that they would require ten square metres (twelve square yards) for each person. Even in the largest rock shelters there are unlikely ever to have lived more than about thirty persons at one time as a larger

53

number would have had to range over too wide an area to find veld food. Hunter gatherers require a great deal of space. In the Kalahari it amounts to several square kilometres each and even in the well watered Drakensberg, would have required about one or two square kilometres per person.

The cases of paintings superimposed on others have been mentioned and the reasons for this practice will be discussed later with other problems. One suggested explanation is that it was done to express a meaning. The simplest explanation is that the best 'canvasses', having regard to protection, good rock and accessibility, and perhaps other considerations, were already taken up; so the later artist just painted over the early art. But is this true? Please satisfy yourself on this. Are there as good surfaces left unpainted as the ones overpainted?

But enjoy the paintings chiefly as art. Note the sensitive line and delicate shading, by no means easy to achieve on a roughish rock face, the skilful depiction of action, especially in the human figures, the cases of perspective and foreshortening, the composition. Don't miss the miniatures. There are a few cases where a natural feature, a crack or bulge, has been used as part of the picture, and some where the artist has fitted his painting to a natural frame.

You will notice that, apart from the children's art, which is not very common, work below a certain, and fairly high artistic standard, does not appear, or very rarely. No doubt that artists had to be competent to be 'hung' in the salon, but how did they learn the manual skills? These are not instinctive and require much practice. Again we do not know!

You will form your own opinions of the art as such. For one person to tell another what to admire is an impertinence — though the critics do it all the time. And the finer qualities of an art defy verbal description. As I have said elsewhere 'the peculiar function of art begins where the powers of language end'. Or as Proust said it affords us "the revelation, which would be impossible by direct or conscious means, of the qualitative difference there is in the way the world presents itself to us, a difference which, but for the existence of art, would remain the eternal secret of each individual."

8. SOME PROBLEMS

You have (I hope) now read the foregoing and have seen a good sample of the art. You know what the Bushmen painted and how they painted, the question now is *why* they painted.

When the cave art of Spain and France was discovered, and in the face of the most obstinate scepticism was finally accepted as the work of Palaeolithic man done about 30 000 to 12 000 years ago, the same question was asked. It was observed that many of the animals painted were shown stricken by darts and spears. In a famous case the clay modelled body of a bear that once no doubt had a bear-skin placed over it, had thirty deep holes in it. These facts gave rise to the view that the motive was magic, that it was believed if an image of an animal was made, whatever was done to it would happen to the beast represented when next it was hunted. This was supported by the fact that belief in sympathetic magic was worldwide. It was part of witchcraft in medieval Europe and is sometimes practised even today, for example in Voodoo rites and the 'black magic' cults being revived. Even now in Australia some rock paintings are made for the purpose of 'puri-puri' or death sorcery. The procedure there is to obtain something from the body of the intended victim — hair, a sweaty garment, or excrement — and bury it in the floor of the cave, then to paint a figure, usually horizontal, to represent the person, chanting a curse the while. The intended effect is supposed to begin as the painting is completed.

In the European Palaeolithic cave art paintings of gravid animals are fairly common and this is seen as another kind of sympathetic magic — for promoting fertility and therefore increase. The almost total absence of representations of human beings there could be explained as being forbidden in their culture as it would give the artist similar powers over humans, and this, like witchcraft in Europe, would be prohibited.

How far can this idea be used as providing a possible motive for the Bushman artists? Not very far! Pictures of dead or dying animals are found, but comparatively rarely, perhaps two or three per cent of the whole number of animal paintings. Also there is nothing in their folklore, as far as it is known, or in their present practices to suggest a belief in sympathetic magic. On the other hand the animals most often painted were those they preferred to hunt — the big game — not the small ones which probably provided as large a part of their actual diet; and it might be that the artists, or some of them had an idea, perhaps unconsciously, that painting chosen animals gave them some power over them. But, you will say, this will not explain the painting of human beings, which actually outnumber the animals. No! But it *could* explain why the animals were painted realistically, likeness being of the essence of sympathetic magic, and the humans were much stylised. The one was hunting magic and the other was not, it was to depict the many activities of their culture, memorable dances, historic fights, a major trek. Also there might well have been a taboo on realistic pictures of humans: otherwise why did these skilful artists *never* make anything like a portrait — of a girl or a parent — face as well as body.

How to explain the virtual absence of paintings of plants in the 'Berg? There are some of them, but only a few, in other art regions. On the theory that the painting of animals was part of food-getting magic why not paint plants also and promote their increase. It is accepted that plant foods provided a large part of their diet as it does in the Kalahari still. There are at least thirty plants in the Drakensberg, parts of which, seeds, fruits, leaves, roots or tubers, are edible. The answer might be that these foods were easily come by, magic was not needed. Anyway to collect them was womens' work and the artists were apparently male. Their food getting activity — hunting — was a worthier subject. Male chauvinism is not a recent development.

There is an alternative explanation to regarding the animal paintings as serving a function, as being a part of the food getting process, and that is the art for art's sake or art *pour l'art* theory, that the artists painted for pleasure they had in the exercise of their skill and showing it off to their little community, and that they considered the animals to be beautiful and as such fit subjects for their art. I will revert to this point.

The predominance of antelope as painting subjects, and of the eland among the antelopes, can be accomodated by either the food getting, or the *art pour l'art*, theory. Antelope were a preferred source of meat as one kill would feed the whole band, and the eland, which may weigh up to 900 kg (2000 lbs) and has much fat on its body, would ensure many days of ease and plenty. But they are also beautiful animals, again especially the magnificent eland, and by most artists now would be preferred as subjects to the other animals present — dassies, hares, rats, et cetera. Antelope would also be the ones of the larger animals most commonly **seen.** The cats and the nocturnal animals seldom would be and the small ones only fleetingly.

It is accepted that the artists put more effort into the paintings of eland, in artistic technique and size as well as in numbers, and the animal features largely in Bushman folklore. This had led to the thought that there was a further reason for its being a special subject: that the 'Berg Bushmen had a religious attitude to the animal. The full argument for this theory is given in Patricia Vinnicombe's *People of the Eland* (See 'Further Reading'). Both she and David Lewis-Williams argue that the animal paintings must be symbols. The latter writer also takes the eland paintings as evidence for this but the rather metaphysical argument cannot be dealt with briefly and should be read as presented *(Lewis-Williams 1982)*. I disagree with his theories on the general grounds that they are more elaborate than is necessary to explain the existence of the art. The chief objection to the idea of symbolism is that where a symbol is adopted, and often repeated, it tends to become progressively simplified. If the eland was painted, as suggested, as a symbol for some other desirable thing, then any recognisable representation of it would do. The development in the art of the paintings of eland took the opposite course: they started as simple monochromes and bichromes, then became polychromes and finally evolved into the shaded polychromes, painted with much detail and in varied and difficult attitudes.

The idea of symbolism has also been used to explain the attachment to the penis shown in the human figures and mentioned in Section 1:3. The suggestion is that it symbolised a prohibition on sexual intercouse (before a hunt for example) or on urination while hunting. A study of the many examples, however, shows it to be common in many of the activities depicted, dancing, fighting, walking, or apparently inactive, as well as in hunting scenes. And here again the objection applies that if what is shown was symbolic one simple form of it would suffice, indeed would be better, whilst it actually appears in a multiplicity of forms, for example a single, double or triple bar and with or without various attachments. It is a mystery, but most probably represents something attached directly to the organ as an ornament. The Bushmen, unlike the Hottentots and Bantu, are not known to have worn the penis sheath. For a thorough study of the questions see Willcox (1984) in 'Further Reading'.

We come to the problem of the superimposed paintings. If it was done only because the best 'canvasses' had been taken then the problem vanishes *(Section 1:7)*. If there were equally good ones unused, the question remains; but it might have been that one part of the shelter was 'the salon' having good lighting and the best floor, and the other parts the kitchen, or nursery. It has been noticed that the paintings tend to be 'thickest' and most superimposed when the wall backs a good area of reasonably level floor and which was presumably the 'sitting room'. Assuming that the superimposing was not because of lack of available space equally suitable from all points of view, why was it done, and fairly commonly? One study showed that about nine per cent of paintings were involved, either as the lower or the upper painting.

If the later artist merely wanted to supercede the other painter, to be 'one up' so to speak, he had two ways of giving himself a clear field. One was to take a piece of sandstone and grind the paint off the surface, the other to put a wash of paint over it which would also serve as a good base for his own painting. I have found no signs that he did either of these things and this is rather strange as the older painting, as far as it remained exposed, did somewhat mar the effect of his own. Perhaps it was simply not done to efface another man's work but alright to paint over it.

There are other theories. One suggests a practical reason: that the lower paintings acted as the 'primer' for the upper one, preventing uneven absorption and also saving paint. This can be dismissed. Very few of the upper paintings cover more than a portion of the lower one. Quite often the upper is, for example, a large eland superimposed on a small figure or figures. If the intention was to use the older painting as the primer, the later painter would have looked for one which could contain his own or nearly so. The overlap is often very small.

One researcher has thought to show by statistics that some kinds of paintings were more frequently involved in superpositioning than others, and that some of these were painted on older ones more often than they were painted upon. This he concluded was deliberate and must have some significance. The study however did not properly apply probability theory nor did it take size into account. Given a total painted surface large paintings are more likely to be involved either as the lower painting on the top one, than are small ones. When this factor is taken into account and probability theory is applied, the placing of certain kinds of paintings, e.g. eland, rhebok, humans, on other is seen to be a random process as far as the selection is concerned.

In Australian aboriginal art the rock paintings accepted as done for magical purposes are stated to be often painted upon others and it is thought to indicate a belief that their 'magical potency' would thereby be increased. It has been suggested that this might have been the case in South Africa but there is no real evidence to support the idea. If it was believed then surely the superimposing artist would plant his painting fairly and squarely over the other. But this is rare: the average is about a forty per cent overlap and is often much less.

None of these theories, even if accepted, throws much light on the question of artistic motivation. It has been mentioned that one study shows only about nine per cent of the Drakensberg paintings to be involved in two-element superpositioning. Now the case of superpositioning was created by the artist who painted the top one — the earlier artists cannot be supposed to know what might happen in the future — so only about 4,5 per cent of paintings were intentionally involved, leaving about 96 per cent not so involved.

An interesting question arising from some of the paintings of eland is whether the Bushmen attempted to domesticate this animal. The fact of domestication of animals was observable by them for many centuries from their first contacts with the Bantu with their cattle and sheep. Eland have been successfully domesticated in South Africa and elsewhere. You may see many paintings that show Bushmen apparently walking peacefully with eland (but beware of false grouping!). A few seem to show ropes attached to eland and one case clearly shows a bound animal. It is quite feasible that the Bushman should have herded the animals at least to the extent of keeping them confined to a convenient valley. We shall never be sure of this, but it is worth looking out for examples in the paintings as evidence.

A question which has probably occurred to you is how the artists could paint animals so naturalistically from memory. They could hardly take an eland and much less an elephant or leopard into the cave as a model. I have suggested that the artists, or some of them, had what is called the eidetic faculty. There is good evidence for this (see my *Rock Art of Africa*). This enables its possessor to record in his 'minds eye' a very vivid picture, recall it at will, and, as it were, project it onto a surface in order to draw it. It is quite different from an ordinary memory image and it can be held and inspected in detail. This would explain much in the art. How they could paint those difficult attitudes and why panoramic scenes are absent — a wide angle view cannot be recorded eidetically.

Another question now under discussion is whether the Bushmen stayed in the 'Berg during the winter or whether at least some of them moved down to the midland plains or even to the coast at that season. They could not have done so after the coming of the Black men and the White but it would have been possible earlier.

Some of the game animals no doubt moved seasonally up and down the 'Berg but others would remain, especially small game, but also such animals as bushbuck and mountain reedbuck. Vegetable foods would be less abundant in winter, but seeds and bulbs could be stored.

Paintings of herds of eland showing bulls, cows and calves together indicate a summer scene and paintings of pre-mating or mating behaviour, by eland and rhebuck for example, may indicate spring if the paintings were of actual herds — in which case the artists were there also at these seasons. But there is no reason to doubt this; the question is whether they remained there in the winter. It is a difficult question on which archaeology might throw some light by identifying animal bones in cave deposits in and below the 'Berg.

To return to the question of motivation, in scientific matters the fewest and simplest hypotheses that will explain the facts are to be preferred to more complex and far fetched ones. What are these? My own conclusions are that some paintings were made as records of actual events; this seems beyond argument in the cases of the historical scenes, the White men with their guns and wagons fighting Bushmen or hunting. Most of the group scenes can be taken also to be records of pleasant or important events in the life of the community or the artist's personal experience. This would include trance experiences. Some, there is no reason to doubt, illustrate myths, like pictures in our children's books. As for the animal paintings to which most artistic effort was devoted, some idea of gaining influence over the animals portrayed might have been in the artist's minds, but it is simpler to suppose that they were painted for the pleasure of seeing recreated on the rock wall what gave pleasure at first sight.

But what was the underlying motive? What moved them to learn the arts of the painter, procuring the ingredients and making the paints, and by a great deal of practice mastering the techniques? Only, I think, pleasure in the acquisition and exercise of skill with the added satisfaction of being admired (and perhaps rewarded) for it.

Once only was the question 'why do you paint?' put to a Bushman artist, not in the 'Berg but in S.W. Africa/Namibia, and the answer (translated) was 'for the pure pleasure of representation'. This I believe was basic but other purposes, discussed above, were added.

RESORTS

1. NATAL PARKS BOARD PARKS AND RESERVES
(listed alphabetically)

Bookings for **hut accommodation** must be made with the Reservation Officer at the Natal Parks Board Headquarters, Queen Elizabeth Park, P.O. Box 662, Pietermaritzburg 3201 telephone (0331) 51514, telegraphic address 'Fauna'. For **Campsites,** however, bookings are made with the Officer-in-charge of a particular Reserve.

In the Drakensberg these are:

Hillside Camp, this is 30 km (19 miles) from the hutted camp at the Giant's Castle Game Reserve, address Hillside, P.O. Box 288, Estcourt 3310, telephone (03631) 24435.

Himeville Camp Site, at Himeville Nature Reserve adjoining the village, P.O. Box Himeville 4585, telephone Himeville (03392), ask for 36.

Loteni Camp Site, Loteni Nature Reserve, P.O. Box 14, Himeville 4585, telephone Himeville (03392), ask for 1540 during office hours.

Mahai Camp Site, Royal Natal National Park, P.O. Mont-aux-Sources 3353, telephone (03642) and ask for Mont-aux-Sources 3.

Rugged Glen Nature Reserve, this adjoins the Royal Natal National Park, and the address and telephone number are the same.

Visitors to the hutted camps must bring their own food and drink: provisions are not sold at the Reserves.

Some rock paintings in the Reserves have been damaged by visitors or have had names and dates written near, and even across, paintings. Because of this the Parks Board has regretfully decided that not all painting sites should be made generally known and shown on the local maps. Some sites have been fenced and have a locked gate for access which will be opened by a Game Guard or guide who will conduct parties to the sites at arranged times, and remain present during the visit. Wardens or Rangers in charge may, at their discretion, direct persons to other painted shelters which will be mentioned hereunder and in Section 3. Visitors in charge of children are requested to keep an eye on them: they are the chief- but not the only — culprits in writing their names in the shelters, and should not be allowed to go alone to them.

Giant's Castle Game Reserve

The beautiful valley of the Bushman's River in which the hutted camp is situated constitutes, with the adjoining land, the area probably the richest in prehistoric rock art in the world. I would think undoubtedly so if quality as well as quantity is taken into account. If you look under almost any rock overhang you will find paintings. For the new-comer to the study of Bushman art it is perhaps the best place to start as there are two of the larger painted caves (The Main Caves) only about a mile away. One of them has been turned into a museum with wax models of a Bushman family in realistic attitudes. The caves have been fenced in but a Zulu guard is present during the day to admit visitors under his eye. He has a taped description of the paintings and the historical background which is turned on once an hour if visitors are present.

Based on the hutted camp is a Ranger Naturalist well informed on the Bushmen and their art as well as the wild life of the Reserve. He will answer questions and will conduct suitable parties to certain of the painting sites, notably Bamboo Hollow, Steel's Shelter and Willcox's Shelter. The route to Bamboo Hollow passes close to the Elephant Shelter which might also be visited. *(See Section 3 for descriptions).*

Himeville Nature Reserve

The Reserve has ten campsites with ablution facilities and may serve as a base for visiting the rock paintings described under the headings Sani Pass Hotel *(Section 2c and Cobham Forestry Station Section 2b).*

Injusuti Hutted Camp

This Reserve forms the northern end of Giant's Castle Game Reserve but is reached by a different route. Proceeding from the Estcourt direction pass the Loskop railway station and you will see the Injasuti signpost on the left 6 km further on. Coming the other way cross the Little Tugela Bridge and only about 1 km further you will come to the sign. A rough road leads you for 32 km through a portion of Kwazulu territory to a truly beautiful spot.

This is the resort from which to visit the famous Battle Cave *(see Section 3).* This shelter has been very properly fenced off and can only be visited with a guide. The procedure is that at 9 a.m. every day, weather permitting, those wanting to go will be conducted to the cave. The walk is 8 km (5 miles) each way along an unspoilt valley, climbing about 240 metres (800 ft). Take lunch and don't hurry. You are very likely to see eland on the way along and possibly other buck, and almost certainly baboons. Leopards still exist in the area. On the way, on request, the guide will show you 'Copulation Rock' near the path in which a scene, so interpreted, is painted. This is one of the very few scenes of human copulation, or of animal mating, in the paintings. Battle Cave should be your first priority.

A map is obtainable, gratis, from the Camp office which shows the paths leading to two other rock shelters with paintings. One of them, with only a few remaining paintings, is part of a row of shelters at the very top of the Cave Sandstone called Grindstone Caves because what looks like a millstone, round with a square hole in the middle, is to be seen in one of them. The walk is about 6 km (4 miles) each way with a gradual climb of about 240 metres (790 ft). You will not be deceived by some 'paintings' in black done by some joker in the cave with the grindstone with a piece of charcoal — thereby demonstrating his artistic inferiority to the Stone Age artists. The real paintings are in the furthest of the shelters but they are few.

First as you approach are two human figures each with one leg lifted, perhaps dancing. Then a single eland in a yellow ochre and white with shading. A good touch is the **shadowing** of the top of the two 'off' legs. Beyond the eland are three figures with some objects on their shoulders.

The shelter called Fergie's can also be visited. It is about the same distance as Battle Cave but up the other fork of the Upper Injasuti stream. On one of them is a scene of about 30 figures dancing around a large red 'ball' of uncertain interpretation. Some fakes can be seen.

You are permitted to sleep in the Grindstone Cave and Fergie's Cave but not to light fires in them or any other rock shelter.

Visitors to Poacher's Stream Cave, also shown on the Parks Board map will note some paintings on the right of the cave, almost all human figures in various attitudes, or eland. Few are in good condition and some of the clearer ones are of doubtful genuiness.

A painting site on the south slope of Wonder Valley is shown on the Natal Parks map. It is about 6 km (4 miles) each way and has only a few paintings, but among them are two good shaded polychrome eland, also other buck and human figures of the usual kind. There has been some vandalism and crude imitations, probably by white children.

Kamberg Nature Reserve

The accommodation comprises a hutted camp and the Stillerust converted farmhouse and rondavel.

The only rock paintings known in the Reserve are at the Waterfall Shelter — very faint and hardly in themselves worth a visit. They are, however, next to the path leading to one of the finest painted shelters in South Africa, the Game Pass Shelter. This is one of the fenced sites but you can be conducted to it by a guide provided by the Ranger in charge. See Section 3 for description.

The Waterfall Shelter, formed in Molteno Sandstone, gives little protection to the paintings. There are faint traces of a buck in red, two bichrome eland, and a small group of human figures in red, one in a bowing posture.

Adjoining the Reserve, higher up the Mooi River valley and on a side stream are several shelters with well preserved paintings, some of them of considerable interest also for their subject matter. These are on Forestry Land but entry may be made from this Reserve with a permit obtainable at the hutted camp. The valley land immediately adjoining the Reserve is a privately owned farm to be passed through only by permission, or to be by-passed through the Forestry Reserve.

If possible the shelter known as the Kranses should be visited (see Section 3). A walk of about 6 km (3,7 miles) each way is required. A little further on is Nuttalls Shelter, and others in the vicinity are Christmas Cave, Willem's Cave and Sandra's Shelter.

Loteni Nature Reserve

This Reserve is approximately 76 km from Nottingham Road on the Himeville road turning off at the Loteni Store. The hutted camp comprises 12 bungalows, two cottages and a larger cottage.

There is an abundance of wild life and good fishing, and beautiful scenery, but only one painting site with a few paintings, not very clear and of no special interest. The Officer-in-Charge will direct the enquirer.

Royal Natal National Park and Rugged Glen Nature Reserve

This Reserve with the adjoining Rugged Glen Nature Reserve is world famous for the grandeur of its scenery as well as its wildlife. It is not well endowed with notable rock art sites although the last sighting of a band of 'Berg Bushmen took place here in 1878.

Only one painting site is shown on the good coloured map obtainable at the Parks Board office and shop. This is a shelter in the Sigubudu valley about half an hours walk from the road at the nearest point, and the path is well sign posted. Because of damage partly natural and partly by vandalism the Parks Board has had to place a fence a few feet from the rock face, but what remains can still be seen and photographed. A frieze high up and just under an overhanging mass of rock is still reasonably clear. From left to right there are human figures in various attitudes, an indistinct animal, a small rhebuck partly painted over a feline (probably a leopard), then three eland in faded polychrome. Below are masses of paintings of which little can be distinguished. To the right at about eye-level are faint remains of a spirited dance scene. This was fairly clear when copied by a member of a German expedition in 1928 and even when photographed by me in 1952 but little can now be seen. Still further to the right is an eland in yellow.

There are a few paintings in a very small shelter formed in an isolated rock 5-10 minutes walk from the Tendele Hutted Camp in the Vemvaan valley. Here also little remains clearly visible but you might make out a figure running 'flat-out' behind an eland, five other human figures, the tallest about 20 cm (8 inches) holding a bow, and two faded polychrome eland.

Another painting site, of considerable interest, is near Sunday Falls but because of possible vandalism it is not desired by the Park authorities that it be generally known and visited. This may be possible, however, by arrangement with the Warden who will then provide a guide. The rock shelter is not easy of access. For description see Section 3 under 'Sunday Falls'.

Vergelegen Nature Reserve

The turn-off to this Reserve is 16 km north of Himeville on the way to Nottingham Road and there is another 19 km to reach the huts. The accommodation consists of two 5-bedded cottages.

The Reserve has much to offer the nature lover and the fisherman but it has little for the rock art addict. Only one site is known, directions to which should be sought from the Officer in Charge of the Loteni Nature Reserve.

·The group of paintings is on a fallen rock in a small rock shelter and comprises three horses with riders. The two leading riders appear to be Europeans with guns and the third an African ('Bantu') with a knob-kerrie. This probably dates from 1860 when there was Commando activity here against Bushman raiders; but although so late the paintings are not well preserved.

FORESTRY STATIONS

A large number of the painted rock shelters of the Drakensberg are on the Reserves of the Directorate of Forestry; and the Directorate was responsible for compiling the excellent map described in the Preface (page x). The map, however, shows only those caves in which overnight camping is permitted: some having paintings, others not. The resident Forestry officers do not offer guided excursions within their territory but may give detailed directions, on request, to anyone wishing to visit a particular spot, whether an archaeological site or otherwise.

If you are visiting a Forestry Reserve please note the following:
You may not be on Forestry land without a permit, which is obtainable from any of the entry points, and from certain of the hotels nearby. A permit is also required to enter any Reserve controlled by the Natal Parks Board and this is obtainable at the entry points and offices. By a useful arrangement the two organisations also issue permits into each other's adjoining territory so that you may enter, for example, a Forestry Reserve and on a long hike pass through and exit from a Parks Board Game Reserve. Whatever the entry point you will be required to fill in a 'Rescue Register' stating your route and intended length of stay. When you leave, the time and date must also be entered in the Register.

If you intend to stay overnight in one of the caves where this is permitted you must 'book' the use of it at the Reserve entry point. This cannot be done in advance. Printed in brackets with the name of the cave on the Forestry map is a figure which indicates the recommended maximum number of persons that can conveniently stop over for a night. Twelve is the upper limit for any hiking or camping party. Note that you may not camp in any other caves than are shown on the map, and you must not light fires in a cave or anywhere else in a Reserve.

The above restriction may seem irksome, but they are necessary in order to preserve the wilderness character of the 'Berg.

The hotels adjacent to the Reserves are shown on the key map and listed in *Section 2:3*. Camping facilities at each Reserve will be described hereunder. Camp sites may be booked ahead, with payment in advance, by calling at, or writing to, the Forestry Station concerned. The addresses are as follows:

State Forest	Address	Tel code & No	After hours
Cathedral Peak	Private Bag XI Winterton 3340	03682/3621	3622
Cobham	P.O. Himeville 4585	03392/1831	

Garden Castle	P.O. Box 90	
	Underberg 4590	03372/1722
Highmoor	Private Bag 51	
	Rosetta	033332/1322
	3301	
Mkhomazi	P.O. Lower Loteni	033312/1902
	3281	
Monk's Cowl	Private Bag X2	03682/2204
	Winterton	
	3340	

Cathedral Peak Forestry Reserve

Camp sites served by ablution facilities are provided. Two of the caves shown on the Forestry map, in which camping is permitted (see above), have rock paintings; these are Poacher's Cave and Leopard Cave.

Poacher's Cave is one of the more habitable caves in the Ndedema valley and best approached from below the steep zig-zag part of the path down the valley and following the base of the krans towards the head of the valley. It has more than 200 independent painted figures excluding a swarm of bees on the extreme left of the cave spread over a wide area. Although tiny, many of them are clearly painted in two colours. What is probably a bees' nest is also shown next to the remains of a human figure in a kaross who might be under attack.

The rock is exfoliating and only fragments remain of many paintings. On one exfoliated area is a good clear painting of a reclining reedbuck, one of the few such in the 'Berg. In front of its head is a horizontal line which might represent an arrow about to strike. Further to the right are human figures, with fairly high up a good little scene of two hunters closing in on a buck and loosing their lethal arrows. Not much else is clearly visible on the rock face but there are other paintings on fallen rocks including a group of five felines.

The Leopard Cave is further down the valley to the east of, and not far from, the path. It has well over a hundred paintings but they are mainly fragmentary. In the right hand portion of the cave there are some eland in faded polychromes, three of them lying on their backs, presumably killed, with hunters standing by. Some distance to the right is the scene which gives the cave its name, a feline chasing a 'flat out' running man.

Other notable painted caves in the Reserve are the Sebaaini Cave in the Ndedema Gorge, Junction Shelter, the Eland Cave, Ladder Cave in Rainbow Gorge, Knuffel's Shelter in Masongwane Valley, and the Xeni Shelter in the Umlambonja Valley. For descriptions of these see Section 3.

Cobham Forest Station

This station is reached by taking the D 7 road towards the 'Berg from the southern end of Himeville Village. It is situated on the Giant's Cup section of the Drakensberg Hiking Trail which extends from a point near the Sani Pass Hotel to the Police Post at Bushman's Nek. It is one of the overnight stopping places with a building which can accommodate up to 30 persons and provides bunks with mattresses, tables and benches, and certain utensils. Camping along the trail is not permitted, nor sleeping in the caves. The trail leading south from the Station passes within a few metres of two caves with rock paintings.

Only about 20 minutes walk along the trail is the Cobham cave, a large one but with only a few paintings. They are on the 'ceiling' near the entry point and are best seen by climbing on to a fallen rock. The paintings comprise several eland in polychrome without shading.

A further walk of about an hour leads on to Bathplug Cave, a huge one so called because the water which normally falls from the top flows back into the cave and through a large hole in the floor. It is formed in Molteno Sandstone of very coarse texture which does not provide a good 'canvas' for painting. As the cave is normally damp there is efflorescence and some growth of lichen on the rock face. The artists therefore did not attempt large paintings but adapted their work to the very small areas of suitable rock. Entering the cave from the left all the paintings appear to be in the first 20 metres, beginning from a fallen rock about 10 metres in and extending a further 10 metres. There are hundreds of tiny stick-like human figures mostly in black, but some in red, in all sorts of expressive attitudes — running, dancing, gesticulating. At about 5 metres from the fallen rock are several paintings of horses, some with riders, and below this to the left the remains of a polychrome eland. A further metre along look for a bunch of 'pin-up girls' with marked steatopygia.

The Forest Station is the point of departure for visiting the Mpongweni Shelter (also called Sepongweni) perhaps the finest gallery in the Drakensberg considering quantity, clarity and interest of the paintings. It requires a strenuous walk of about three hours to reach it and two to two and a half to return. The shelter is in the Cave Sandstone and it is interesting to compare the paintings there with those on the Molteno at Bathplug Shelter to note the effect of the rock on the art produced. Some of the paintings in each — the horses — must be about the same age. For description see under Mpongweni Shelter.

Garden Castle Forest Station

This Station is approached from Underberg. It provides camp sites (tents only) with toilet facilities, and although a guide is not available the Forest Officer will give directions, aided by a local map, to two painted shelters. These I have not visited — see what you make of the paintings yourself. A report would be much appreciated.

Highmoor Forest Station

For the last few kilometres the road is very bad in places. Basic camping facilities are provided.

Directions can be obtained from the Forestry Office for visiting a small shelter only about 200 metres away, a larger one near the road about 2 km (1,2 miles) down the valley, and by a long walk others in the upper Mooi River Valley. For the latter see under Kamberg Nature Reserve.

The near paintings, on bad rock, include a polychrome eland in a fair state of preservation and a few faint human figures and other buck.

The rock shelter down the valley is very long but shallow and also of bad rock. Remains of many paintings, mainly eland, will be seen high up on the rock, and on projecting masses two groups of rhebok in a fair state. The last group of paintings you will come to is a group of figures, one with a bow. Above it is a long legged animal of uncertain species.

Mkhomazi Forest Station

Coming from Nottingham Road the Station is a distance of approximately 39 km, just after crossing the bridge over the Inzinga River. From the Station it is a walk of about 2 km to three rock shelters close together usually called the Cyprus Caves from the old farm name. The Forest Officer will give directions. They are not shown on the Forestry map.

The paintings are of considerable interest and in order of approach are as follows: A group of three figures wearing the animal head and skin hunting disguise or ritual garb. The legs are clearly human. One (top left) was apparently not completed. The figure at bottom with a wide bead necklace and long neck is painted over two small buck and has superimposed the fore part of an eland in polychrome — making three layers of paint — apparently unrelated. The middle figure also shows beads around the neck and has horns faintly visible. To the right of it is a similar figure very much smaller. Above the group are several tiny black human figures in action which might or might not be part of the scene. Immediately to the right are a number of figures possibly forming part of the same mysterious composition. About ten stick figures in orange and white circle about a figure in dark brown which from its general shape and legs appears to be a prostrate human wrapped in a kaross: the attention of the stick figures is upon it. This might be a burial scene: the explanation applicable elsewhere that the figure is a collapsed dancer does not seem to fit here. Above is what looks like bits of an uncompleted animal, and to the right of it another of the head and skin clad human figures similar to the ones above described and possibly showing that they are part of one ensemble. This figure holds a bow in front of it confirming that it is a hunter dressed up; and the head shows a tusk. It wears, as it were, a 'crown' of up-turned spikes. The kaross is fringed and the neck again is beaded. Here you should form your own opinion of the whole panel. Representational, purely imaginary, a trance scene, a true whole or in part false grouping?

Monk's Cowl Forest Station

This Station has camping facilities and caravan sites and is a good starting point for some of the long walks necessary to reach the large painted caves between the Station and Cathedral Peak area — see under Cathedral Peak Forestry Reserve. Remember the necessary formalities.

For nearer sites see under Champagne Castle Hotel.

3. HOTELS
(listed alphabetically)

Below the tall figures is a double row of human figures to a much smaller scale walking along ground lines. Some wear karosses and carry bows, quivers and other objects.

There are about thirty other figures, mostly of the usual kinds, but you might spot a group of humans in faded black apparently in combat. As one holds a spear and another and axe these are no doubt representations of Bantu.

There is no doubt that the sad deterioration of these paintings is due to the proximity to the stream which enabled visitors to obtain water to throw on the paintings to make them show up. Please don't do this, it is vandalism and is illegal.

Also nearby is Buy's Cave to which a guide can be provided or an excursion arranged. See under Mountain Splendour Caravan Park and for description of paintings *Section 3*.

Bushman's Nek Hotel

Address: Bushman's Nek Hotel,
P.O. Box 137
Underberg
4590
Telephone: 03372/103

The management organises an excursion with a guide to two painted shelters on Forestry Land, requiring a total time of about six hours for the round trip. One drives about 3 km to the Police Post where entry permits are obtained. The first part of the route is easy walking along a track leading to Bushman's Nek Pass and on to Sehlabathebe in Lesotho, but the rest of the walk is rougher going.

The first shelter is about two hours walk and is of medium size with very clear paintings. On the extreme left are faint remains of paintings of indeterminate kind. Near the centre of the shelter about 2 metres (6 ft) up is a group of polychrome eland overlying human figures. Towards the right are several layers of super-imposed paintings difficult to disentangle, mainly in polychrome with human figures predominating. Three human figures march to the right, and one large man leans forward holding a bow. There are several other similar figures in this attitude which is probably part of a dance. Near the top of the panel of paintings are some typical eland in polychrome and near the bottom two rhebok in white shown one behind the other.

Above the panel is a 'tall' human figure in white with red touches and having the penis attachment, and two smaller figures to the right of him.

At the right end of the shelter is a group of figures in white with animal-like heads-probably the hunting mask. One of them holds a very long stick with a small unidentifiable animal on the end of it. This probabl represents the method of hunting burrow-living animals mentioned in Section 1:3. Porcupine quills were noticed near the shelter. Below and to the right are some typical kaross clad figures, one of the birdlike figures with 'streamers', and a figure with a baboon-like head and arms resembling an eland's legs. Below again and on the underside of a projecting mass of rock are a number of human figures leaning forward or running, and one seated in frontal aspect with knees up.

Lack of time and a slight accident (to my wife) prevented us from visiting the other painted shelter accessible from the hotel. There you are on your own.

Cathedral Peak Hotel

Address: P.O. Winterton
3340
Telephone: 03682
ask for Cathedral Peak 1.

Among the attractions of this hotel is that you may combine enjoyment of the grand scenery with visits to many painted rock shelters. A coloured map can be purchased at the office which will help you find the rock art sites (although not specifically marked upon it), and a guide can usually be obtained.

One of the nearer sites is called Procession Shelter. To get there takes about three-quarters of an hour by the path across the Umlambonja River, through part of the plantation and on to a point just below Baboon Rock. As you approach, look down to your right and you will see a large detached rock right on the bank of a small stream with some trees next to it. On the stream side is a small shelter. Very conspicuous on a light patch of rock are nine quasi-human figures, the tallest about 30 cm (1 ft). They are shown with animal heads and with what appears to be furry bodies yet they wear bands of beads at the waist and knees. Hovering over them is one of the mysterious winged creatures, here bird-like.

Below the tall figures is a double row of human figures to a much smaller scale walking along ground lines. Some wear karosses and carry bows, quivers and other objects. There are about thirty other figures, mostly of the usual kinds, but you might spot a group of humans in faded black apparently in combat. As one holds a spear and another an axe these are no doubt representations of Bantu.

An excursion conducted by the hotel is to the Bushman Pool. About 2 km (1,2 miles) east of the Forest Reserve entrance a path leads to the left down to the pool in the Umlambonja River. A cliff overhangs the water to form a rock shelter. It is the only one I know from which the Bushman occupants could have fished seated at home. Enough remains of the paintings to show that they were numerous — probably several hundred — and some of them of exceptional interest and beauty: but now they are very faint.

From left to right you might make out two human figures in red, then four in dark brown. About 1,2 metres (4 ft) to the right is a group of three beautifully shaded polychromes of rhebok only about 76 mm (3″) in length and hardly visible. Immediately above them is the beginning of a row of about 40 human figures all in different attitudes, walking, running, dancing, gesticulating. Round a sharp corner of the rock are two reclining figures leaning backwards, two bird-like creatures with long tails and to the right of these a mass of hardly visible paintings.

There is no doubt that the sad deterioration of these paintings is due to the proximity to the stream which enabled visitors to obtain water to throw on the paintings to make them show up. Please don't do this, it is vandalism and is illegal.

The painted shelter on Mushroom Hill is approached along the path to Doreen Falls. When facing the Falls you will have a steep slope on your right at the top of which in the first band of sandstone is the cave. For description of the paintings see under Mushroom Hill Cave in Section 3.

The hotel serves as a comfortable base from which to visit the rock paintings sites of the Ndedema Valley and Knuffel's Shelter in the Masongwane Valley, in the Cathedral Peak Forest Reserve *(see Section 2:2)*, also Junction Shelter and the Eland Cave, somewhat further afield. You can drive a large part of the way by proceeding up Mike's Pass in the Reserve.

To reach another interesting painting site known as Ladder Shelter take the path from the hotel leading to the Indumeni stream and Rainbow Gorge. This is Route II in the hotel guide booklet: and see hotel map. Just before reaching the gorge cross the stream, climb out and traverse the steep slope on the other side. You will soon see the cave in the band of sandstone above you. This walk requires some effort, and is best undertaken with a guide by arrangement with the hotel. For description see 'Ladder Shelter' in *Section 3*.

Cathkin Park Hotel

Address: Private Bag
Winterton
3340
Natal
Telephone: 03642 ask for Cathkin Park Hotel 1

Small rock painting sites can be visited from this resort by a morning's or a day's walk. They are shown on the map pinned up at the hotel and a guide can be arranged for. The nearer rock shelter is called Buy's Cave but because of extensive falls of rock only a few remain. The walk takes you up 'Skeleton Gorge' so called because of remains exhumed there of people who were identified as 'Bantu' with some admixture. There are several paintings of human figures in the cave in expressive attitudes and one faint animal. Small people who can get under the fallen rocks have reported a few more. See *Section 3* for fuller descriptions.

A further shelter is called Anton's Shelter or Theodorous after the original farm name and is on the edge of the Little 'Berg. Although a longish walk a visit is well worth the effort for the view alone. There is a good dance scene. At top left is a seated woman (with typical fat buttocks and thighs), and other women, with their collecting bags beside them. A little below and to the right is the dance, a *pas seul* in which a man wearing a headdress and holding two sticks leans forward in the 'all fours' attitude to imitate an animal's movements. He is nearly surrounded by people, mostly women, clapping the rhythm. A man with a bow-case and stick walks in from the right. He has the penis attachment. There are a few other human figures to the right.

For sites further afield to be reached from this Hotel, see also under 'Champagne Castle Hotel'.

The Cavern Berg Resort

Address: Private Bag 626
  Bergville
  3350
  Natal
  Telephone: 03642/172

This resort is a good base from which to visit rock art sites on the property, on adjoining farms and in the Royal Natal National Park. Conducted walks are arranged to four painted shelters. Three of the sites are shown on the Resort map.

One of the sites is the Cannibal Caves. The paintings are few and faint but a visit is well worthwhile because of the historical interest. The caves were the home of cannibal Amazizi during and following Chaka's wars against other Natal tribes when the defeated, deprived of their cattle and driven from their fields, resorted to the practice. The caves are undoubtedly those referred to by J.W. Mathews in his book *Incwadi Yami* visited by him in the early 1880's. Cannibalism was also rife in Lesotho as attested by Government Agent J.H. Bowker in 1869. It might have been as late as this that some of the paintings showing Bantu were made. The paintings at the site are only a large eland, about 56 cm (22 inches) long superimposed on red human figures, with some other similar figures adjoining. Another site, the Baboon Cave, has two of the finest animal paintings in the 'Berg, both vaal rhebok, a buck and a reclining doe with head turned back *(Plate 26)*. They are only 8 cm (3 inches) overall and beautifully shaded. Also in this shelter is a group of three rhebok in white and yellow, even smaller, being about 5 cm (2 inches); traces of two felines; and other faded paintings.

Chalmer's Shelter is remarkable for a procession of about a dozen dumpy figures shown as wearing bird-like masks over their heads. There are some other human figures of the more usual kinds, and two running felines, from their build possibly lions.

Another painting site known as Lone Rock has numerous little running figures in red, some with bows and other equipment; an animal of uncertain species; and a good little fight scene with two groups of Bushmen confronting and shooting arrows at each other.

For neighbouring sites see under Royal Natal National Park.

Champagne Castle Hotel

Address: Private Bag X8
  Winterton
  3340
  Natal
  Telephone: 03642 ask for Champagne Castel 3

This beautifully situated hotel is well below the Cave Sandstone so the painted rock shelters nearby are small ones in other rock strata. The map hung on the wall near the office — copies of which can be purchased — shows the positions of the shelters. Easy to find even without a guide is the one called Maartens Shelter. It is a little more than a mile from the hotel and about 150 metres to the left of the main path. The shelter is a very small one formed in a huge lump of Cave Sandstone which has detached itself and rolled down the slope.

Most of the few paintings are now faint — it is surprising that any remain visible with so little protection from the elements and exposed as they are to veld fires sweeping into the shelter. On the left and low down is a delightful group, still quite clear, of grey rhebuck, a buck facing three does. The painting of the heads is especially delicate. To the right of the group are two small buck in red, another in bichrome, and several human figures of the usual stylised kind, in red.

There are two other small occurrences of rock paintings within easy walking distance which would be difficult to find from a description. The hotel will arrange for a guide if desired.

A somewhat longer walk will take you to some paintings on the further side of Wonder Valley — see hotel map and description under heading Injasuti Hutted Camp.

For the strenuous the hotel is a good base from which to visit larger painted shelters over the Little 'Berg, properly equipped for at least one night out. See Sebaaini Cave, Eland Cave and Junction Shelter in *Section 3*.

Drakensberg Gardens Hotel

Address: Drakensberg Gardens
      4591
      Natal
      Telephone: Drakensberg Gardens 1.

Approached via Underberg this hotel is well into the mountains. Three Bushman Caves with paintings are shown on the local map, all on Forestry land but able to be visited with the necessary permit. I have not yet been able to do this myself so I cannot report in detail.

El Mirador Hotel

Address: Private Bag
      Winterton
      3340
      Natal
      Telephone: 03642 ask for El Mirador 3

This hotel arranges to conduct parties to the neighbouring rock painting sites for one day excursions and by minibus to Giant's Castle Game Reserve, the Injasuti Hutted Camp *(see under these headings)* and the Cathedral Peak Forestry Reserve within walking distance of the Ndedema Gorge *(see Sebaaini Shelter)* and Junction Shelter.

The near sites, reached by driving part way then walking, are the Sterkspruit Valley Shelter *(see Dragonpeaks Caravan Park)*, Black Ox Shelter *(see Mountain Splendour Caravan Park)*, the Wonder Valley Site *(see under Injasuti Hutted Camp)* and Buy's Cave *(see under Mountain Splendour Caravan Park.)*

Himeville Hotel

Address: Himeville Hotel
      P.O. Himeville
      4585
      Telephone: 03392/5

In addition to being the nearest hotel to the Himeville Nature Reserve it is also the nearest to the National Monument rock painting site Mpongweni Shelter *(see Section*

3). To reach the latter turn off at the southern end of the village on to the D 7 district road to the Cobham Forest Station from where the walk begins *(see under that heading).* Other rock shelters with paintings are easily visited from the Station.

A visit to the Himeville Museum is well worthwhile for those interested in the prehistory and history of the area. The museum has a collection of copies of rock paintings from the neighbourhood and elsewhere — the McGuffie Collection — and various Bushman artefacts.

Hotel Walter

Address: P.O. Box 12,
        Bergville
        3350
        Telephone: Bergville 03642/12

This hotel is a good centre from which to make excursions into the 'Berg, especially to the Royal Natal National Park and the Cathedral Peak area. For rock art sites see under Royal Natal National Park in *Section 2 : 1,* Cathedral Peak Forestry Reserve in *Section 2 : 2,* Cathedral Peak Hotel and the Cavern Berg Resort in *Section 2 : 3.*

Little Switzerland Hotel

Address: Private Bag 661
        Bergville
        3350
        Telephone: 03642 ask for Little Switzerland.

This hotel is situated on the spectacular Oliviershoek Pass. It is a pleasant and convenient base for excursions further into the mountains.

Two or three kilometres down the Pass and near the road is a long but rather shallow rock shelter with many paintings. It is on privately owned ground and the owner's permission is necessary in order to visit the site. This can sometimes be obtained by the hotel management. For description see *Section 3* under Oliviershoek Shelter.

Mont - aux - Sources Hotel

Address: Private Bag 1,
        Mont-aux-Sources
        3353
        Natal
        Telephone: 03642 ask for Mont-aux-Sources 7.

For painting sites to be visited from this hotel see under Royal Natal National Park in *Section 2 : 1.*

The Nest Hotel

Address: Private Bag X14
        Winterton
        3340
        Natal
        Telephone: 03642 ask for Nest 2

The management of this hotel arranges for excursions on foot or on horseback to various rock shelters including Anton's Shelter *(for description see under Cathkin Park Hotel)* the Eland Cave, Sebaaini Cave *(see Section 3)* and others in the Ndedema Valley.

There is a rock shelter with a few paintings on Cathkin Farm only 3km from the hotel of which distance 2km can be travelled by car. The shelter is a small one facing east and the paintings are now faint, partly as a result of damage by veld fires. From left to right look for a group of human figures in white. One of them has the penis attachment mentioned in *Section 1 : 3.* Next there is a very faint buck, a striding human with some small buck superimposed, some traces of paint, an animal resembling a feline with a black standing human figure painted over it and some tiny seated humans to each side of the standing figure, one indistinct human figure and finally three rhebok in white, the clearest paintings in the shelter and well painted.

Royal Natal National Park Hotel

Address: P.O. Mont-aux-Sources
3353
Telephone: Bergville 03642 ask for No 1

For painting sites to be visited from the hotel see under Royal Natal National Park in *Section 2 : 1.*

Sani Pass Hotel

Address: P.O. Himeville
4585
Natal
Telephone: 03392 ask for 29 or 30

From this hotel two paths leading to painted rock shelters have been marked out with coloured stones placed at intervals. Descriptions of the routes can be obtained from the Reception Office. A permit must also be obtained as these shelters are on Forestry land.

The shorter walk, along the Gxa-Lingene River, takes about an hour going and half an hour returning, and leads to two shelters about 200 metres (220 yds) apart. They are known as the Good Hope caves after the original name of the property. Sad to say very little art remains visible and none of it is clear, partly because of bad rock and partly because of vandalism. The walk, however, is well worth while, especially for anyone who has not seen a Bushman habitation.

The first shelter to be reached is a very large one and has the further interest that an archaeological excavation has been made in its floor deposit. Radio-carbon dating indicated that a Later Stone Age people lived in the shelter as long ago as 7 600 years ago. Others using the kind of stone implements the Bushmen used (the so-called Smithfield N) were here more than 2 000 years ago and painting may well have been practiced from that time. With these stone artefacts a bone fish-hook was found, showing that they were also fishermen. The few remaining paintings include, to the right of the centre of the cave and about 60 cm (2ft) above the floor, two horses with riders and remains of others. Further to the right some human figures in red can be seen.

In the second cave more paintings are visible and a few are fairly clear. From left to right look for the following. Behind a small tree (at the time of writing) one horse in red and part of another. About 6 metres (20ft) to the right and 1,5 metres (5ft) above the floor a horse in red and black with a black rider. About 3 metres (10ft) to the right in a kind of alcove there are several layers of faint paintings including one buck in white, several indeterminate animals in red, one of them upside down, and some human figures in red, one with a bow and quiver. Further on only about half a metre (1'7") above the floor two hartebeeste in red can be seen and on the extreme right of the cave a horse in white is still clear with a standing human figure wearing a long kaross above it.

The horse paintings at these caves must date from the 1850's and their poor condition must be blamed on visitors who wet them to make them temporarily more visible. This is wickedly irresponsible as well as illegal. Some paintings recorded in 1956 have now completely disappeared.

The other painting site, on Ikanti Mountain, requires a longer walk — about 2½ hours out and 2 hours back — with some steep going. But it has some of the clearest rock paintings in the 'Berg. For description see *Section 3* under 'Ikanti Shelter.'

Another of the finest galleries, Mpongweni, is in the vicinity and is reached by first driving to the Cobham Forest Station and then walking. See under that heading.

Underberg Hotel

Address: P.O. Box 28
Underberg
4590
Natal
Telephone: 03372/22 Underberg

This is a good base from which to visit rock painting sites at the southern end of the Natal Drakensberg especially the Mpongweni Shelter; and see other sites mentioned under the headings Cobham Forest Station, Sani Pass Hotel, Bushman's Nek Hotel, and Drakensberg Gardens Hotel. It is also a good base for trout fishermen.

White Mountain Resort

Address: P.O. Box 609
Estcourt
3310
Telephone 03631-24437 Estcourt

This pleasant family resort is well placed for excursions to see the rock paintings of the Giant's Castle area — see under Giant's Castle Game Reserve and Injasuti Hutted Camp in *Section 2:1*. The former requires only half an hours drive and the latter about an hour and a half.

Among excursions arranged by the management is a morning's enjoyable walk to the Fern Cave — a rock shelter with a fine show of various ferns behind a curtain of falling water — and a small painted shelter close by called Angus's Shelter after its discoverer. The paintings are few and some of the most interesting, near the top of the rock face, are now hardly visible. They include a 'tall' human figure followed by a stooping figure wearing an animals skin as hunting disguise. Below and to the right are clear figures — a standing figure with a bow, but with the head missing, one of the small mysterious winged creatures, another small human figure, and a crudely painted animal which might be intended as an antbear.

CARAVAN PARKS

Dragon Peaks Caravan Park

Address: P.O. Winterton
3340
Natal
Telephone: 03642 ask for Dragon Peaks No. 1
After hours 03682/3713

This well known resort is off the Champagne Castle Road 4 kilometres from the hotel. A map is obtainable from the store showing the walks in the neighbourhood and some rock painting sites.

The nearest is the Sterkspruit Valley Shelter which can be visited by the courtesy of the landowner. It is only about 3km up the valley along a rough road. Organised walks and rides to it are arranged or a guide (not really necessary) can be obtained.

It is a small shelter with little protection for the paintings which are few but interesting. All are of animals with no human figures that I could see. Nor is the usual eland represented: the antelope are rather stiff bichromes of hartebeeste — note the reclining one near the top of the panel — and tiny, beautifully painted buck of uncertain species. One of these, also at the top, only about 5cm (2 inches) is shown side view but with the head turned forward. Even to this scale the legs are painted in two colours and the ears are clearly detailed — a little masterpiece especially as the rock is rather rought Molteno sandstone. At the left is the rear end of an elephant in white: the head has disappeared.

Also nearby is Buy's Cave to which a guide can be provided or an excursion arranged. See under Mountain Splendour Caravan Park and for description of paintings *Section 3.*

Kelvin Grove Caravan Park

Address: P.O. Box 31
Winterton
3340
Natal
Telephone: 03682-2502 Winterton

This caravan park lies at the foot of the mountain called Arthur's Seat off the Bergville to Loskop Road. About two-thirds of the way up the mountain is a band of sandstone in which a rock shelter is visible from the Park. Directions or a guide to the best route will be given. The going is difficult just before reaching the shelter because of tangled bush and erosion of the slope.

The shelter has only a few paintings but they are of considerable interest. There are some long-legged, animal headed, quasi-human figures and several fo the mysterious creatures which might illustrate trance experience. One of them is clearly winged with feathers indicated and others have long streamers flowing backwards from the presumably flying creatures. Among them is a seated figure with an animal's head, legs far apart, and knees up. He appears to be sitting on a stool but it might be a back apron spread to sit on. The figure has some resemblance on a smaller scale to the one in Willcox's Shelter at Giant's Castle and another in a small shelter in the Ndedema George. *(Fig. 20 F & G)*

Further to the right is a group of three figures in crouching or stalking attitudes. At the bottom of the panel of paintings is a tiny figure holding a bow with an arrow ready to shoot.

This resort is well placed for excursions to the Cathedral Peak and Giant's Castle areas as well as for visits to local sites.

Mountain Splendour Caravan Park

Address: P.O. Box 178
   Winterton
   3340
   Natal
   Telephone: 03682-3503 Winterton

This resort is reached by turning left half a kilometre after crossing the Sterkspruit Bridge on the Champagne Castle road.

This park has only a few, and small, painted shelters nearby but is a convenient base from which to visit others further afield, for example those in the Injasuti area and within the Little'Berg. The local sites, however, are well worth the walk — itself enjoyable.

The owner will conduct parties personally, or provide a guide, to the Wonder Valley rock shelter *(described under Injasuti Hutted Camp)*, the Sterkspruit Valley Shelter *(see under Dragon Peaks Caravan Park)*. Another small shelter on the farm Diodlof can be visited. It is called Black Ox Shelter from the subject of one of the paintings, of which there are only a few. There are also some small buck in red.

The cave must have been somewhat noisy to live in as there is a waterfall over the top of it.

Buy's Cave, which can also be visited, is at the bottom of the north slope of the ridge which is parallel to and north of the Sterkspruit (see map obtainable from Dragon Peaks Caravan Park). It is within walking distance of Mountain Splendour, Dragon Peaks, and El Mirador, or one can drive to within about 2km. The cave is large but with only a few paintings remaining, partly because of rock falls and partly because of vandalism. *See Section 3* for description.

The painted cave called Theodorus or Anton's Cave can also be visited as a conducted excursion driving first as far as the byroads will take you and then walking up 'Jacob's Ladder' onto the Little 'Berg and along the top of the sandstone escarpment. See under Cathkin Park Hotel for description of the paintings.

In visiting these sites it should be remembered that you are on private property by the courtesy of the owners. Please keep to the paths, do no kind of damage, leave no litter and above all light no fires.

ROCK PAINTING SITES

Bamboo Hollow, Giant's Castle Game Reserve

This site is an easy walk of about 6 kilometres (3,7 miles) from the hutted camp.

The shelters are formed by slight overhangs and have only a few paintings, but some are clear on good rock.

In the first shelter you approach (Bamboo Hollow 1) from left to right you will see, around a corner of the rock three rather indistinct figures, two of them wearing the medium length kaross. Then there are four clear figures walking towards the right. They may be wearing short capes or it may be portion of a kill slung over their shoulders. The two middle figures show bows above their shoulders. They have some kind of headdress. Below them is an uncompleted animal painting, and above to the right one of the mysterous winged creatures (see Section 1:3) with a human bending over it.

Further to the right is the main scene in this shelter in which several men wearing unusual headdresses surround an animal which looks most like a bull of the native Sanga breed (fig 5). One of the figures seems to be holding a spear and about to give the coup de grace to the animal which is shown perhaps bleeding from the mouth. There is definitely a spot of paint below the animal's muzzle. It is an odd scene as the presumed hunters do not have bows. At top right is another of the winged creatures. This is one of the cases where they could be regarded as the departing anima of the dying beast: but how then to interpret the similar one near the four marching figures far to the left and mentioned above. If you look closely you will see a line of tiny crosses upwards from the animal's withers: this is of uncertain interpretation.

This scene has been interpreted by Dr J.D. Lewis-Williams as the killing of the mythical rain-animal as seen by an artist-medicine man in a state of trance. I prefer the simpler explanation, hunters making a kill of a bull stolen from Bantu and driven, very possibly, near to the very spot to be butchered. The animal does not look at all like those accepted as depictions of the rain animal.

Note in the animal the sophisticated artistic touch of disconnecting the two 'off' legs, see Section 1:5.

About 50 metres to the south along the krans at Bamboo Hollow 2 is a painting of about 20 figures similar to the ones above described. To the right of them is a typical collecting bag. Further along are two more groups of paintings less clear but worth a close examination.

Battle Cave

This is a medium sized rock shelter with not much living space. It is one of the most remote, requiring an 8km (5 mile) walk, each way, from the nearest resort which is the Injasuti Hutted Camp of the Natal Parks Board. For this reason it was probably one of the last to remain occupied and it has some of the clearest paintings. There are about 700 including fragments.

The scene to which it owes its name is a fight between two bands of Bushmen, probably over hunting rights in the much restricted territory still available to them *(Plate V)*. It is full of action and detail, and it may well depict an actual attack by an invading band on the occupied shelter. That the defenders are on the left is shown by their having women with them; the attackers would leave theirs at a distance. Some of them are shown leaping into the fray or running in the expressive 'flat out' manner. The attackers run in from the right except two who have been hit by arrows. One of them walks out bleeding from the arm and another lies also bleeding from the arm, and from the head. There are no casualties among the defenders who presumably drove off the attack, remained in possession and painted the picture. Note the arrows flying through the air. One of the attackers is unusually detailed *(Plate 15 & fig 9A)*. He has white painted stripes spiralling his legs and a large quiver full of arrows; and he holds his bow and two arrows in one hand while apparently signalling with the other of which even the fingers are shown. The arrowheads are of flat triangular iron type used only towards the end of the Bushmen's life in the 'Berg. There is a touching detail on the extreme left where two would be warriors were being held back by women grasping their arms. Perhaps they were too young! *(Plate 14)*

The fight scene is at the right end of the shelter. If you start from the other end you will see, high up, a little group of lions and two elongated animal headed figures, a very clear bichrome feline *(Plate 19)*, probably a leopard although it has no spots, and a polychrome eland browsing off some leaves. Do not miss on the side of a projecting mass of rock two animals in white and red with tusks. *(Plate 20)*. Some take these to be rhinos but I think they are bush-pig boars with their two curved tusks. See what you think.

Towards the centre of the shelter there is a mass of superimposed paintings of animals and humans and above it a group of eland. To the right is a group of rhebuck in two lines, and next to it (and rather faint) the rear end of an elephant and one ant-bear both in white. To the right of these and high up is a frieze of three insect-like creatures and two animal masked figures, one waving the animal tail implement, superimposed on a bichrome eland *(Plate 16)*. Then other masked figures and animals. Near the right end and low down are two good steatopygous Bushwomen with digging sticks, and a third which looks like a child's attempt to copy them.

Among the great many other paintings are some figures wearing what looks like West African 'devil masks'.

You should allow yourself plenty of time at this cave.

Buy's Cave

This large cave had paintings at two levels which I will refer to as the lower and upper friezes. Largely owing to vandalism by irresponsible idiots who also wrote their names, very little remains of the lower frieze.

On the upper frieze from left to right (east to west) there are faint traces of eland in yellow and white, a large animal in black and white and three red running humans with the action well shown. The clearest remaining group is above a pointed fallen rock: five seated figures face to the right. Four of them wear karosses painted in yellow. To the right are four figures in action.

Probably this is a dance and the seated figures the women audience. Between the seated and dancing figures are two indistinct animals superimposed. To the right again some other figures are running towards the dance.

Somewhat to the west are paintings on the underside of a large fallen rock almost certainly painted when the rock was part of the face. An eland in red, another in yellow and some black human figures and some in red can be made out. Under another fallen rock is a painting more like an elephant than any antelope.

This cave was one of those visited by the German expedition led by Leo Frobenius in 1928-1930 which copied and published the scene of the seated figures and dancers. I can see no deterioration in this group.

Christmas Cave

The paintings in this small shelter are on its ceiling in three or four superimposed layers. An eland apparently never completed partially covers two cloaked figures. Another human with a prognathous head and without a kaross has a large quiver full of arrows. Above this group are three thin bird-like figures. To the right are a delicately painted rhebok, an eland in foreshortened rear view, a bichrome eland in lateral aspect and minute animal figures climbing up a slope.

The Eland Cave

This is the largest of the painted caves *(Plate II)*. It is situated on the south slope of the Mhlwazini valley between the side streams Ndedema and Nkosazana and faces approximately north-east. It is not easy to find so a guide from one of the hotels is recommended. This is the cave in which, on the high ledge you will see, a Bushman hunting outfit was found. The paintings run to over a thousand so plenty of time should be allowed.

It was named because of the group of eland near the centre of the frieze of paintings *(Plate III)*. The biggest is a shaded polychrome in unusually bad proportion but partly superimposed upon it and to the right are many smaller eland polychromes in good proportion and various attitudes. The large eland is superimposed upon human figures and a roan antelope (rarely portrayed), so there are at least three layers of paintings here *(Plate III)*.

Above is a panel of paintings with more eland over running human figures and, to the right, seated figures next to two small huts *(Plate 10)*. In the extreme right part of the cave are some bush-pigs in shaded polychrome, the technique generally reserved for eland.

The cave has paintings far too numerous to be described in detail. They are much superimposed. Some figures are drawn from myth or were painted to illustrate trance experiences *(see page 35)*. Such are two 'flying buck' and some similar figures with two streamers flowing from them. There are rows of figures wearing long karosses. Some paintings have baffled interpretation. There are many paintings of humans high up on the wall with action well depicted. In the left (south) part of the shelter look for a small winged object, perhaps a moth, and some concentric curves probably representing a beehive *(fig 12A)*. Look on the underside of all projecting masses of rock or you will miss paintings. Some uncompleted work will be observed showing the painting technique.

For some colour illustrations see Willcox (1956) in 'Further Reading.'

Elephant Shelter, Giant's Castle Game Reserve

Only about 4 km (2½ miles) from the hutted camp this shelter has poor rock largely encrusted with lime and has only a few clearly discernable paintings. These are the small group of elephants, in dirty white, which gives it its name, and one animal with them which looks like a tapir (which is impossible): it might be a sheep. To the right is a reclining man in red with the penis attachment and at least three baboons, also in white.

Note especially towards the right end of the shelter a very delicate painting of an eland in white.

Close examination will reveal a few more paintings, rather indistinct.

Game Pass Shelter

This famous rock shelter must be approached via the Kamberg Nature Reserve as it can only be visited accompanied by a Game guard or Forestry employee. The walk takes 1½ to 2 hours each way and the last part of it is steep going, but it should not be missed. It has some of the the clearest paintings in the Drakensberg which must be among the latest although there are no definitely datable paintings here such as scenes including horses. They must, however, be well over a century old proving how well the Bushmen knew how to make paint.

The site has long been known and a photograph of some of the paintings was published in *The Colony of Natal Railway Guide* in 1895. It was this photograph, showing figures wearing long cloaks, which came to the notice of Professor R.A. Dart in 1925 and led him to believe that they were representations of foreigners 'cloaked Asiatics of the Babylonic-Phoenician period', i.e. well over 2000 years ago. The Abbé Breuil accepted this interpretation. Professor Dart did not visit the site but the Abbé Breuil did, in company with the late Professor C. Van Riet Lowe, and it is difficult to understand how he could have believed these extraordinarily fresh looking paintings to be of such an age.

The shelter is a long one facing north. Starting from the left end you will see two ploychrome eland, one of them shaded, then a small elephant in red about 8cm (5") long, and above it some parallel curved lines, rather faint, which probably represents a bees' nest as they have been shown to do so elsewhere.

A few metres to the right is a frieze of paintings comprising several figures wearing karosses. They have the highly conventionalised prognathous heads common with such figures and wear bead necklaces. The leading figures clearly carry small buck, showing that they are returning hunters. They could represent Bushmen but rather more probably are Bantu of a friendly tribe such as the Amazizi. At the end is a scene of a Bushman with bow and arrows about to shoot at a buck in red. Continuing to the right after a gap there is another frieze. First a figure in frontal aspect with horns like those of domestic cattle; then a remarkably clear shaded polychrome eland in lateral aspect but with head turned forward *(Plate 24)*. Oddly in such a detailed painting the horns are not shown. An elongated quasi-human painted in orange grasps the eland's tail: his feet, or rather hooves, are shown crossed. He is one of three orange figures. The middle one appears to be bowing to the one on the right but might possibly be dancing in the 'arms back' position mentioned in Section 1. One writer *(Lewis-Williams see Further Reading)* believes the unusual position of the eland's feet and the hair standing on end to indicate that the animal is dying, and the three figures to be part of a trance scene. Whether the whole group has an esoteric meaning depends, in

81

the first place, on whether they form one scene or whether the figure holding the eland's tail was added by another artist with humorous intent. That the eland and the figures are in different colours lends some weight to the possibility. Eland driven to the point of death are said to bleed from the mouth or nose and this is sometimes shown in the paintings: but not in this case. This is another controversial group of paintings. Note the curious running figure on the 'ceiling' above the orange figure.

Next comes the principal group of paintings which comprise at least three layers of paintings *(Cover & Plate X)*. First to be painted was an eland about 1,5 metres (5ft) long which is now faint but the line of the back and withers can be seen. Then shaded polychrome elands and the cloaked figures — again with conventionalised animal-like heads. The latter are the one's referred to as having been thought to be foreigners. Some of them are clearly under eland paintings but others appear to be over them — it is not quite clear. If under and over they must be taken to form part of a scene, men mingling with eland. This could indicate partial domestication of eland or may, of course, be a purely imaginary scene. At least the men and the beasts seem to be about the same age and the shaded polychrome technique is generally agreed to be a late development, fairly certainly within the last three centuries. Above these paintings is a line of tiny running figures in red with touches of white — one is unfinished — which appear to be the latest of the series. To the left of the main group are other eland and, higher up, small human figures one of which has the penis attachment.

To the right of the main panel is a miscellany of eland and kaross wearing figures. Partly superimposed on one of the eland is a good example of a hunter wearing the animal head and skin stalking disguise: below the waist he is obviously human.

Ikanti Shelter
This shelter is reached by following the demarcated path from Sani Pass Hotel. It is a small one but the paintings are numerous and clear. The main scene *(Plate 7)* comprises about ninety figures marching to the right. They differ in detail, some being naked and others wearing karosses. Most of them carry equipment — bows, quivers, bags, sticks or bunches of arrows. One would suppose this to represent a migrating party but the marching figures all seem to be male. Only one figure, right at the top of the group, and seated, is clearly a woman. So the men must be off to some all male jamboree or to war — which latter is very unlikely. Over to the right in the second row of figures from the top you will notice one with and exaggerated penis and the attachment before mentioned. In front of him is the most detailed figure, wearing a cap and a medium length kaross, and having beads at his knees shown by minute dots *(fig 6D)*. A bunch of arrows shows at his shoulder.

Below the main scene, and probably unrelated, are some similar figures walking the other way: and near the bottom of the painted rock face some others sit around animal kills.

Near the extreme right of the main scene two small paintings of rhebuck should not be missed: they are two of the most delicate in the 'Berg *(Plate 27)*. Just below and to the right of them are rows of finger dots — possibly a tally. How many rhebuck we killed this year?

Junction Shelter
So called because it is near the confluence of the Mhlwazini and the Ndedema. It is

south-east of the actual junction and high above the stream. It can be reached by following a path from below or by branching off from the path down the Ndedema valley. A guide is desirable.

It is one of the most habitable shelters, of good size and a level floor, some depth, and facing north with a fine view along the Mhlwazini valley, so it is not surprising that it has over a thousand paintings, counting all traces.

The most interesting painting is the scene of a rope bridge with men crossing it (fig 13A). It is well known that the Pygmies could make such bridges but not that the Bushmen could. It is low down on the extreme right (north end) of the shelter. The ends of the supporting ropes are attached to stakes and two men are running across from right to left. Note that the bridge sags a little where the feet touch, as it would do in fact. To run across such a bridge is rash and one person has apparently fallen off it. The other figures I do not read as part of the scene but as dancing, waving their tail-on-stick implements while the two women on the left clap the rhythm. But what do you think?

But the cave is chiefly remarkable for the preponderance of human figures. Some are painted very elaborately with red streaks on white bodies, presumably depicting body paint. There are some good dance scenes and other activities with plenty of action, and over to the left a spirited baboon hunt — the men using clubs, the male baboons standing to fight while the mothers flee, babies on backs.

Above the bridge is a group of human figures, seated or dancing, with all their equipment, bows, quivers, bags and two lots of digging sticks.

The penis attachment is very commonly shown in this shelter and there are many of the mysterious winged creatures, some animal-like, some bird-like.

Some of the humans have animal heads.

There is much over painting, no doubt because the good rock is limited in the shelter.

Knuffel's Shelter
This painting site, also known as Rhebok Shelter is in the Masongwane Valley in Cathedral Peak Forest Reserve and should be approached through the Reserve entry point. It is a small shelter up a steep slope and is partially obscured by bush.

Almost all the paintings present are of rhebok and comprise one scene (Plate 25). They are bichromes in red and white with some shading. It is clearly the mating season when these buck, normally seen in groups of three or four, come together to form herds of twenty or more. It is a delightful scene with the animals in many attitudes, playing, courting, and in one case, it seems, fighting as the males will at this time. To the left and high up is one of the very few mating scenes, a buck mounting a doe.

To the left of the main scene is a good clear painting of a reclining buck fitted into a small area where the rock has exfoliated.

There are only a few human figures and these are of the usual kinds, running and seated.

The Kranses, Kamberg Area
This is one of several painted rock shelters within easy walking distance of the Kamberg Nature Reserve. They lie in, or adjacent to, Game Pass Valley which is also the name of one of the farms. The site may also be reached from the Highmoor Forest Station by a longer walk. For more information regarding the route see under that

heading as well as under Kamberg Nature Reserve.

The shelter is long and rather shallow but with some hundreds of paintings, many of them still fresh looking. Bushmen were still living here and raiding down the valley in the early 1870's. At the deepest part of the shelter in a kind of alcove there are some paintings of special interest (Plate 2). A procession of figures marches to the left. Some apparently carry shields and must therefore be Bantu. Perhaps they are Amazizi, a Bantu tribe which lived on friendly terms with the Bushmen with whom they intermarried. Below and to the right one man bows to the ground before another while a third figure looks on: it has been called 'the submission scene'. Above, some unshaded bichrome eland move left to right and five men carrying bows run in the opposite direction. One is superimposed on an eland showing the men to be later paintings. The group is an example of the contrasting manner of painting animals and humans, the former naturalistically and the latter more stylised, especially, as in this case, when in action. Here the action is well shown and differs in all the figures.

The animal paintings in the shelter are almost all of eland ranging from rather stiff bichromes to shaded polychromes. You may note that in two cases men appear to be walking with eland in a true grouping, suggesting possible herding of this animal.

A group of elongated standing humans in red and black, and elegantly drawn, is also of interest.

Ladder Shelter

This rock shelter in Rainbow Gorge can be conveniently visited from the Cathedral Peak Hotel or through the entry point of the Cathedral Peak Forest Reserve. See the forester for directions to reach it.

The site is remarkable for the number of superimposed paintings in several layers making it difficult to determine which elements belong together and to 'read' the ones partially or wholly covered. There are polychromes of eland and other buck including hartebeest. Some of the paintings of small buck are unfinished and show the stages by which the artists built up their paintings.

Towards the left of the shelter are the paintings of ladders shown in the illustration (fig 12C). Note that the lower one is hung from a stake or peg presumably driven into the rock and the upper one is similarly secured above lines which might include the top of the rock face. The two ladders overlap as if they were not long enough separately so that the climber would have to change from one to the other. A close look at the upper ladder shows a little climbing figure near the top.

To the right among the mass of superimposed paintings is the rope bridge with a figure cautiously crawling across it (fig 13B).

The situation of the cave makes it plausible to suppose that these were pictures of ladders and a bridge actually used. Immediately below the shelter, down a steep slope is a deep gorge cut in the rock with almost vertical sides and only about 6 metres (20ft) across the top. I am suggesting that in order to cross it without going a long way round the Bushmen fixed ladders down one side of it and up the other until someone had the bright idea of making the four-strand rope bridge stretched across and secured to trees or stakes on the brink at both ends.

The evidence for the use of rope bridges here and at Junction Shelter is unmistakable: but for the paintings we would not know that they were made by Bushmen or any other people in Southern Africa.

84

Main Caves, Giant's Castle Game Reserve

These two rock shelters, only about 50 metres apart are among the largest of the painted caves, and easiest to visit, being only about 2km (1,25 miles) along a good path from the hutted camp. As the paintings are numerous, extremely varied, and mostly clearly visible, these caves are, from all points of view, good places to begin a study of the rock art.

The western cave is the larger, with a better floor, and has hundreds of individual paintings, so a detailed catalogue with descriptions cannot be attempted here and only the paintings of special interest will be mentioned.

Near the centre and above a large fallen rock are paintings of various ages superimposed *(Plate VIII)*. The most conspicious are two human figures in polychrome walking left to right. They wear the antelope head stalking mask and the leading hunter carries two killed rhebok, a ram and doe. This painting is superimposed on one of two hartebeests in red. Between the two hunters is a quasi-human figure and next to the head of the left hunter are two tiny figures greeting each other with outstretched arms. One has a baby on her back. To the left is a figure wearing a long kaross and above that is a feline. To the left again are more kaross-clad figures and two good hartebeests.

Leaving the main panel of paintings and going to the extreme left of the cave you will see high up a frieze of eland-lion-eland-lion and a man standing over an upside-down eland. Below this frieze is another comprising bichrome eland and cloaked figures one of whom carries a bow. Near the centre are two eland bulls which have been described as fighting. Eland, however, do not fight like this — they put their heads well down — and they are more likely to be licking ticks off each other or both browsing off the same bush.

To the right of the main panel and lower down is an intriguing procession of about eleven figures with others above them. They wear the knee-length kaross and have animal-like heads with head-dresses, some horned. One at least has a bow showing at his shoulder and two seem to carry large quivers. Others have bulges on their backs which might be portions of their kill.

These people are painted in a manner quite different from the way the Bushmen usually depicted themselves and the prognathous heads and horned head-dresses together with the long karosses probably indicate that they are Bantu, in which case they would be Amazizi as the tribe took to using the bow and no doubt also adopted Bushman hunting methods *(see Section 1 : 3)*. The strangest thing is that they are shown with hooves like those of eland. Is this perhaps fo showing the empathy of Bushmen with eland? It occurs elsewhere and is one of the mysteries.

Towards the right and high up look for two small figures in polychrome. They are very clearly wearing the animal head and skin stalking disguise but the one to the right is quite clearly a Bushman from the waist down. The horns on the heads are shown as those of cattle indicating that these are late paintings as the technique also suggests. They also are shown with hooves or, just possibly, with sandals.

On fallen rocks are an eland painted upside-down (but which does not look dead), another eland in fore-shortened rear view, a good roan antelope, and much else. Over to the right do not miss one of the rare paintings of snakes, probably a python *(Plate 22)*. It is superimposed on a human figure but is not constricting it: the paintings are of different ages. You will also notice some eland in yellow.

Leaving the west cave a short walk leads to the eastern one, where the museum has been established. Right at the back and seen by climbing onto a fallen rock is a procession of figures in light red. They are clearly returning hunters as two of them carry killed buck. Immediately behind the display cases on a large rock are many layers of paintings. Some are of eland but at the bottom is a procession of fifteen figures walking which has been given the fanciful name 'the slave gang'. There is no reason to suppose that they are not Bushmen on trek. You will notice also two inverted cones in light red joined together. This presents another enigma: they could possibly be a pair of drums.

In a cleft between two rocks is a painting of a man with a stick driving an eland towards a tiny crouching figure with a bow ready to ambush the animal *(fig 15)*. This figure is now hardly visible. The running man has the penis attachment.

Further eastward near the end of the fenced enclosure are many small human figures in black. Some holding clubs or sticks have the action well depicted. Low down are probable examples of Bushman children's work.

Mpongweni Shelter

Easiest access to this shelter is via the Cobham Forest Station (which see) but a walk of about three hours and a stiff climb is required to reach it. It is, however, well worth the effort, apart from enjoyment of the walk, as it is one of the larger shelters, and because of its inaccessibility was one of the last to be used by Bushmen, and has some of the clearest paintings. For the same reason, its remoteness, it has escaped the attention of vandals: may this long continue. The site is a declared National Monument and severe penalties attach to any defacement of the rock art. Most of the paintings belong to the 'horse period' from about 1850.

The following descriptions are not necessarily in strict order — one's memory may slip — but the groups should be easy to locate.

Near the left end is a group of five horses, four of them in red and black and the other all in black, without riders. Below these you may see the faint remains of a scene in black showing men standing up in small canoes spearing fish *(fig 14)*. This was clear in 1907 when it was first photographed. The black used by the Bushmen was not one of their most enduring pigments.

Near the above mentioned groups are three 'pin-up girls' in red, with their aprons, and other touches, in black. They exhibit the big buttocks *(steatopygia)* and thick thighs *(steatomeria)* of their race in times of plenty, and they carry digging sticks without weights *(fig 7)*. About here is a good example of a man wearing the head and skin of an animal — from the horns a cow or ox — as a hunting disguise or for ritual purposes *(fig 16B)*.

Next there is a group of three very clear eland in shaded polychrome *(Plate 23)*. Below the one on the left and near the ground is a small figure that looks like a child's attempt to copy the adult work. Above the group there are several human figures in red and black. To the right are a standing figure and two others leaping with very lively action. Both the latter carry two long sticks which could possibly be fish spears. About here is one of the two complex dance scenes in the shelter *(Plate 13)*. A baboon-like figure with a bent tail performs a step in the centre and others dance around, some with feathers in their hair. A little group of females stands to the left, one with a baby on her back. Another woman with a baby and carrying a handbag is at top right. As Patricia Vinnicombe *(see Further Reading)* has pointed out this scene conforms to the description of the Baboon Dance performed by Kalahari Bushmen.

Look now for a group of horses with riders — without doubt Bushmen on stolen horses. One wears a brimmed hat and they hold sticks, or in one case the pronged goad already mentioned. The horses are shown cantering from right to left. Below is a good human figure with an animal head carrying a bow and a knobbed stick.

Next there is the other dance in which several figures — in black and red — perform energetic dance steps, each as he pleases. They all seem to be male, some carry sticks across their shoulders, and several of them have feathers as headdresses. To left and right of the dancers women clap the rhythm. One of them on the right — a black figure — might be playing on a musical bow. This is an excellent example of Bushman skill in depicting movement and avoidance of stereotyping *(Plate XIV)*. Unfortunately water running down the rock face has partially obscured some figures and a circular design of uncertain interpretation.

Near the right hand end of the shelter is one of the best pictures of a Bushman cattle raid *(Plate 6)*. Several figures on foot are driving a herd of cattle and horses to the left. The cattle have variegated markings typical of 'Bantu' owned breeds. The scene is shown in depth and at the top is a horse with rider (probably the leader of the party). He wears a hat and holds one of the pronged goads used to urge on reluctant animals *(fig 9E)*. The horse is well detailed showing the bridle and reins but ridden bare-back. This is probably a picture of one of the many actual raids and it is on the route by which the cattle were driven from Natal into Griqualand East where the Bushmen rustlers were sometimes in league with a Bantu tribe.

There are some other paintings of human figures here and there in the shelter performing various actions.

Mushroom Hill Cave

This small shelter, approached from the Cathedral Peak Hotel, has but a few paintings because most of the rock face is encrusted with lime, leaving little space suitable for painting on. Nevertheless the paintings are of marked interest and well worth the effort to reach them.

Most conspicuous are two quasi-human figures in polychrome *(Plate 17)*. The one on the left is animal-headed and below the waist is elaborately ornamented presumably to indicate body paint. One hand is holding what looks like a tapering stick with a pear-shaped object as part of it. The other figure is also animal-headed and wears part of the skin as a medium length kaross. In one hand — of which the fingers are clearly shown — he holds an object resembling that held by the other figure except it is curved and has two of the pear-shaped attachments. The figures could be interpreted as Bushmen with hunting masks but they have hooves instead of feet which (if not artistic licence) make it more likely that they represent mythical creatures. It is the objects they hold which have aroused some controversy. One could be a digging stick with an unusual bored stick weight but this seems very unlikely in the case of the other which is curved and has two such objects. The way one is held with the thin end apparently to the figure's lips suggests that it, and by inference the other one, are musical instruments of a kind unknown. This is one of the mystery paintings!

Above the two figures are a small animal painting partly obscured by the lime and three human figures shown in the running convention. Below, to the left are some bichrome eland, also partly obscured and above to the left an amusing example of Bushman caricature. A charging leopard has caused two figures to fall head over

heels, others run for their lives, and two seem to cling together in terror.
There are a few other running humans.

Nuttall's Shelter

This shelter is in the upper Mooi River valley — see under Kamberg Nature Reserve. The numerous paintings are much superimposed. Among them near the left end is a 'bogey' animal with gaping jaws and a half human and half animal figure similar to the one in Willem's Cave (which see). At this point there are four or five layers of painting, mostly indistinguishable.

Further to the right look for a good painting in brown and white of a common reedbuck with its forward curving horns (Plate XII), and a reclining doe of less certain species licking her calf.

You cannot fail to note a very spirited scene of running hunters chasing a bushpig which seems to have turned on one of them (Plate XV).

There are a great many other paintings here: take plenty of time and look closely.

Oliviershoek Shelter

This is a long shallow rock shelter formed in Molteno Sandstone and facing North-East. A waterfall flows over the middle of it. Only a few of the paintings are well preserved as the cave has been much used by cattle and their herders, and fires have been made near the paintings.

The clearer and more interesting paintings are, from left to right, as follows. Near the first group of fallen rocks, a buck in white with another in faded red above it, and two paintings probably of domestic cattle in white, the other in white and yellow, both apparently never finished.

Near the remains of a roughly built wall, about 2 metres (6,5ft) up, is a small group of human figures in red engaged in a spirited fight. One of them is so much like the most detailed figure in the fight at Battle Cave (fig 9A) as to suggest the same artist.

Directly above the 'wall' is a large panel of faded paintings including a large polychrome eland, one of the stooping 'arms back' figures thought to indicate a human entranced, (see Section 1:3 & fig 21)) and, at top left, a buck in yellow. Just to the right of this at about 2 metres (6,5ft) above ground are two paintings of wild bees' hives showing the comb. In one of them the bees are shown as dots. See Section 1:3 and figure 12A. A metre to the right at the same height is a frieze of several layers of superimposed painting: at left are three small buck, one painted upside down, below is a steatopygous seated woman and some standing figures in karosses and at bottom a row of tiny baboons each only about 4cms (1½") long. To the right of this group a row of six figures wearing karosses, rather faint except one in frontal aspect showing the overlap of the garment. He has beads around his neck and the animal-like head is turned to the left.

Next to the right are some running humans, one elaborate with a grotesque head. High above (about 4 metres up) are some faint running red figures.

Further on again at about 2,5 metres (8ft) height under a rock projection is a small unshaded polychrome eland with a line of hunters above it.

At the deepest part of the shelter beyond the waterfall at 2 metres (6,5ft) height are two cattle of the Sanga type. The one on the right shows curious markings. Next appear two eland, the one on the right in brown and very well drawn. Below there is a standing human in red. There are, slightly lower to the right, two human figures painted over a faded eland, and other figures holding sticks.

Two or three metres to the right, where the shelter deepens, are the remains of a mass of painting now hardly visible because of smoke from fires, but look for a fine hartebeest in red with black horns.

Sandra's Shelter
This shelter has not many paintings but they include a fine shaded polychrome eland, and the best painting of a jackal so far found in the 'Berg. It is only 7cm (3") long and is clearly of the black-backed sub-species. The animal is shown with front legs extended, the head leaning back with the jaws open, obviously howling. The head is especially exquisite (Plate XI).

At the right end of the shelter and low down are other fine miniature paintings which include various buck, tiny human figures with body paint, and a feline.

Sebaaini Shelter
This is the largest of the painted shelters in the Ndedema valley. Although it is not good from the point of view of habitability — it has a rather small overhang and limited floor space — it has a thousand or more individual paintings, but with the majority only fragments. It is easy to reach by driving from the Cathedral Peak road up Mike's Pass into the forestry reserve as far as the locked gate, then continuing on foot by the path to the head of the valley and down to the crossing of the Ndedema stream. As you go you will see the shelter on the opposite slope of the valley. From just beyond the crossing the path turns down the valley and passes very near the top of the shelter which is the first in the sandstone on the south side of the valley.

The site was one of those visited by a German expedition in 1928, 'lost', and rediscovered by me. This shelter and the others in the valley have been recorded in detail — see Pager 1971 under 'Further Reading'.

The most interesting scene here is a procession of about thirty figures apparently returning from a successful hunt as they wear the antelope hunting masks with part of the skin forming a medium length kaross; and several of them carry buck slung over their shoulders (Plate II). Below the knees the legs are in white making it look as though they wear knee breeches and this is one of the paintings which led to the theory that 'foreigners' were represented. The feet are not shown. There is, however, no reason to suppose that the people are not Bushmen wearing their well known hunting disguise. Some of the figures carry bows and the tops of large quivers of arrows are visible. It looks as though the artist attempted a perspective effect here: notice that the smaller figures are painted with their feet higher up the rock than the larger ones to indicate being in the background.

Almost all the animals shown are eland in the bichrome, polychrome, and shaded polychrome techniques. There are however, one or two hartebeest in the latter technique, a few grey rhebuck, a few buck of indeterminate species, a baboon and two small felines. Notice high up on the rock two clear polychrome eland isolated from the mass of the paintings and to the right of them another in rear view.

There are hundreds of human figures, mainly small, performing all kinds of actions, including two fights. Many of them have the penis attachment. Women are clearly recognisable by their breasts, aprons, and digging sticks.

There is a great deal of superpositioning, in some places five layers.

Among objects shown are two small ladders.

Steel's Shelter

The chief scene at this small shelter comprises a number of polychrome eland apparently being chased by mounted Bushmen painted, with their horses, in black *(Plates 3 & 4)*. On a closer look, however, the eland are seen to be painted in static attitudes, or slowly walking, whilst the horses and riders are in rapid action. For this reason and the general differences of style, scale and colouration I believe the eland were painted first and the scene was turned into a hunt by a later artist, obviously of the horse period. Some of the horses have their action most expertly depicted. Note especially the plunging one on the right with its rider, holding whip and spears, leaning back to maintain balance.

Low down on the rock you will see two examples of Bushman child art, both horse pictures, one much stylised, the other a creditable imitation of the horse and rider mentioned above.

A small area of exfoliation on almost black rock has provided a light 'canvas' for a black painted man in a sprinting attitude, holding a knob-kerrie. He looks like an athlete from a Greek vase of the 'black figure' period — but with action better depicted.

Sunday Falls Shelter

This rock shelter formed in Molteno Sandstone is awkward to reach as it is at the top of a steep and eroded slope covered with thick bush. The paintings are of interest in themselves and because the site was one of those visited by the Frobenius expedition of 1928-29 which copied and published some of the paintings.

Two figures especially aroused the interest of archaelogists, and the famous French prehistorian the Abbé Breuil — judging by the reproduction, he did not visit the site — took them to be representations, not of Bushmen or Bantu but visitors to South Africa from the Near East *(Plate 1)*. He described them as 'persons wrapped in mantles to their knees with wide turned-back collars richly beaded; two of them wear peaked helmets with crests and protection for the nape of the neck. They seem to be carrying sheaves of javelins. They wear garments under their mantles with embroidery coming below their robes'. The figures wear a knee-length kaross. The heads are animal-like but do not appear with the karosses to be the hunting disguise as bead necklaces are also shown. Other beads are shown at the knees (the Abbé's 'embroidery') and at the ankles. Almost certainly these are Bantu with their somewhat prognathous heads caricatured by the artist: the 'javelins', not very clear, the typical light throwing spears used for hunting. The leading figure also carries what are probably fly-whisks.

To the right are two similar figures apparently unfinished. Another figure to the left appears older and unrelated. A good reclining buck is painted over it.

Also of interest are a painting of a snake at least 1,2 metres (4ft) long, a bird-like creature only about 5cm (2") long, two stick-like humans, one with the penis attachment and a group of three other human figures. To the right of the cloaked figures, around the corner of the rock painted in faded red and dirty white is a bee's nest with scores of bees as tiny dots.

Willcox's Shelter

Very conspicuous is the strange figure that rather startled my wife and I when we first looked into this rock shelter *(Plate IX)*. Somebody dubbed it 'the Moon Goddess' for reasons unknown to me, and the name has stuck. Certainly the creature looks pregnant. It has a grotesque head, paws instead of hands, and no feet: is seated 'full frontal' on a stool or possibly a back-apron, with legs up: the legs striped and the body spotted. In one raised paw it holds a bow and two arrows and two bunches of arrows are stuck into a belt around the body. Some of the arrows are shown with broad iron beads which is consistent with the freshness of the painting as indicating a recent date for it.

Somewhat similar figures occur elsewhere in the 'Berg and one must suppose that it is a creature from the lost mythology of the Drakensberg Bushmen.

To the left of the 'Moon Goddess' is a kaross clad figure of a common kind and two excellent and clear running figures, then a group of eland and human figures not well preserved.

To the right of the strange figure is an elephant in yellow ochre, two good striding figures, buck in polychrome, and a clear bichrome hartebeest.

Willem's Cave
This rock shelter has many human figures with action well shown but the best paintings are a procession of eland delicately shaded and a line of galloping hartebeest in red (Plate 18). The legs are only partly shown which increases the impression of speed. The red hartebeest is considered the fleetest of all the antelope.

An interesting group includes a figure on all fours human up to the waist and for the rest animal. It has two heads shown with what might be bleeding from the nose. Similar figures to this occur at other sites, for example Nuttall's Shelter. To the right are four seated humans in rear view.

Xeni Shelter
The Xeni is a side stream of the Umlambonja and the shelter which is on Forestry land can most easily be reached from Cathedral Peak Hotel with the necessary entry permit.

The paintings are few but when I last saw them were clear (Plate VIII). On the left are two grey rhebok in brown and white. Note especially the lower one, shown as if grazing, for its delicacy. The legs about matchstick thin are in two colours. Just to the right is a row of figures standing and seated. Their equipment, sticks, carry bags, quivers, etc., is shown beside them as if seen from above. Above this group is a buck of uncertain kind probably a bushbuck. Over to the right is a rhebok in foreshortened rear view.

HINTS FOR PHOTOGRAPHERS

To photograph rock paintings use colour film. Colour is of the essence of the art and the contrast obtained adds clarity to the photographs.

You will want to take close-ups within 30 cm (one foot): if your camera will not do this you can obtain clip-on lenses which will permit it.

Cameras, nowadays, do everything for you including measuring the light from the camera position. This of course gives an average result over the whole field. I still prefer a hand held light meter with which to measure the light reflected directly off the painting.

I always take and use a tripod in spite of the extra weight to be carried. Although a stout one (my camera is a heavy Mamiya C33 Professional) — it will go in 'telescoped' form into my rucksack. Using a tripod has the following advantages. You can get the exact field you want and hold it while you take the light independently of the camera keeping yourself from affecting the incident light: you can then focus very sharply as you will not be teetering about holding the camera. As the outlines of the paintings are not always sharp you might find it difficult to know when you are at best focus: in such cases I hold a piece of clear print against the rock and focus on that. As the camera is not hand-held choose a small stop with a long exposure. This gives you more depth of field with sharpness and this, especially with close-ups, is important as the rock face will be variously curved.

You will not, however, always be able to use the tripod as a painting of which you want a close-up might be high up on the rock face. I have sometimes had to take such pictures with one foot on the rock and the other on a pile of stones. But a long-focus lens with the camera well back from the painting (to avoid distortion) might do the trick.

You will usually have the light behind you and standing at the camera may effect the light on the object and even cast a shadow. To avoid this use a long cable release with which you can operate the shutter while crouching out of the way.

Colour photography has its special problems. The film is balanced for direct sunlight on the object. In the case of rock paintings this seldom happens and it is unsatisfactory when it does as highlights spoil the picture. In such cases wait if possible until the sun is off the paintings. Generally you will be in a rock shelter with the light coming from a blue sky and your pictures will be affected accordingly. I have found that UV filters of varying strengths will correct this, but selection is a matter of experience. The altitude of the site I have also found to be a factor.

Sometimes I have used a white reflector to throw natural light on to the paintings.

An alternative of course is to use flash which matches the light to the film. I only use it when unavoidable as it can also cause highlights. Most cameras now have flash attachments but this is an inflexible arrangement and I use an independent flash gun on a long cable so that I can vary the position having regard to the stop used.

Sometimes the light will filter through 'bush' in front of the cave or be reflected off a grassy slope. In this case flash is desirable.

Red is the commonest colour in the paintings and some colour films 'warm up' red to enhance flesh tones. This you will learn from experience.

Remember that spraying the paintings with water (or anything else) to make them clearer is not permissible.

The great thing is to know your camera. Note the conditions, light reading, stop and exposure of every shot and compare them with the result.

FURTHER READING

(Listed Alphabetically by Author's names)

Johnson, R.T. — *Major Rock Paintings of Southern Africa.* David Philip, Cape Town, 1979 (Examples selected from the rock paintings of the Republic of South Africa and South West Africa/Namibia for their artistic merit as seen by the author — himself an artist.

King, L. — *The Natal Monocline.* Shuter & Shooter, Pietermaritzburg 1972 (the geology and geomorphology of Natal explaining the origin and structure of the Drakensberg.)

Lee, D.N. & Woodhouse, H.C. — *Art on the Rocks of Southern Africa.* Purnell, Cape Town, 1970 (A general survey).

Lewis-Williams, J.D. — *Believing and Seeing: Symbolic Meanings in Southern San Rock Paintings.* Academic Press, London 1981 (New theories of interpretation with examples from the Drakensberg of Natal and the Barkley East District.)

Pager, H. — *Ndedema* Akademische Druck-u Verlagsanstalt, Graz, 1971. (A complete record of the rock paintings of a single Drakensberg Valley, with discussion).

Rudner, J. & I. — *The Hunter and his Art.* Struik, Cape Town, 1970 (A broad survey of rock art in Southern Africa but more especially that of the south and south-east Cape, S.W. Africa and Angola).

Tobias, P.V. (ed.) — *The Bushmen.* Human & Rousseau, Cape Town 1978. (Authorities write on all aspects of the Bushmen, their physical anthropology, archaeology, history, art, et cetera).

Vinnicombe, P. — *People of The Eland.* University of Natal Press, Pietermaritzburg, 1976. (A thorough study of the rock paintings of the southern part of the Drakensberg of Natal, with the background archaeology and history, profusely illustrated).

Willcox, A.R. — *Rock Paintings of the Drakensberg.* Parrish, London 1956. Second edition, Struik, Cape Town 1973 (The Bushmen of the Drakensberg and their art in Natal and Griqualand East).

— *Rock Art of South Africa,* Nelson, Johannesburg. 1963 (The rock art of Southern Africa, south of the Zambesi, engravings as well as paintings).

— *Rock Art of Africa.* Croom Helm, Beckenham, England 1984. (The rock art of the whole of Africa, from the Atlas Mountains to the Cape, the authorship and age of this art in the various regions, and how the practice diffused through the continent) South African distributors, Macmillan SA (Pty) Ltd. Johannesburg.

Woodhouse, H.C. — *The Bushman Art of Southern Africa.* Purnell, Cape Town. 1978 (The book is chiefly concerned with certain themes occurring in the art with some suggested explanations).

Wright, J.B. — *Bushman Raiders of the Drakensberg. 1840-1870.* University of Natal Press, Pietermaritzburg. 1971 (The last decades of the Bushmen in the Drakensberg — their resistance to invasion of their hunting grounds, their inevitable defeat and extermination).

Many of the above listed books are now out of print so those interested must have recourse to libraries or Africana dealers. For comprehensive bibliographies of the books, papers, and articles relating to the subject see the 'References' in the more recent works listed.

INDEX OF SITES

Page

Angus' Shelter	75
Anton's Shelter	70, 74, 77
Arthur's Seat	76
Baboon Cave	45
Bamboo Hollow	12, 78
Bathplug Shelter	66
Battle Cave	20, 31, 32, 33, 40, 41, 52, 61, 78
Black Ox Shelter	72, 77
Bushman Pool	67
Bushman's Nek Shelter	27, 68
Bushpig Shelter	41
Buy's Cave	70, 72, 76, 77, 79
Cannibal Caves	71
Cathkin Farm Shelter	74
Chalmer's Shelter	71
Christmas Cave	62, 80
Cobham Cave	66
Copulation Rock	61
Cyprus Shelters	67
Eland Cave	18, 22, 23, 35, 65, 67, 74
Elephant Shelter	81
Fergie's Cave	62
Game Pass Shelter	17, 44, 81
Good Hope Shelters	74
Grindstone Caves	61
Highmoor Shelters	66
Ikanti Hill	14, 17, 45, 75, 82
Junction Shelter	24, 65, 67, 72
Knuffel's Shelter	44, 65, 67, 83
Kranses Shelter	7, 62, 83
Ladder Shelter	23, 24, 65, 70, 84
Leopard Cave	65
Lone Rock	71
Main Caves, Giant's Castle	42, 61, 85
Marten's Shelter	71
Mpongweni	13, 20, 24, 25, 27, 30, 43, 66, 72, 75, 86
Mushroom Hill	34, 70, 87
Nuttall's Shelter	62, 88
Oliviershoek Shelter	73, 88
Poacher's Cave, Ndedema	65
Poacher's Stream Cave, Injasuti	62
Procession Shelter	69
Sandra's Shelter	62, 89
Sebaaini Shelter	26, 65, 72, 74, 89
Sigubudu Shelter	63
Steel's Shelter	10, 90
Sterkspruit Valley Shelter	72, 76, 77
Sunday Falls Shelter	6, 63, 90
Tabamyama	29
Theodorus Shelter	70, 77
Vemvaan Valley Rock	63
Vergelegen Shelter	63
Waterfall Shelter, Kamberg	62
Willcox's Shelter	90
Willem's Shelter	37, 62, 91
Wonder Valley Shelter	62, 72, 77
Xeni Shelter	65, 91

NOTES

NOTES

NOTES

NOTES

NOTES

Picture yourself in this beautiful setting

FOR A COLOUR BROCHURE WRITE TO
"THE CAVERN", PRIVATE BAG 626
BERGVILLE 3350, TELEPHONE (03642) 172

Camping or hiking in the Drakensberg?
You should be properly equipped by CAMPCRAFT

Gypsey Sleeping Bag, Size 183 x 83 cms
Weight 1,5 kg, woven nylon outer cotton
inner, folds into bag.

Ontario Tent Size 274 x 274 cms
Weight 18,5 kg, Sleeps 4

Aluminium Framed Rucksacks
Summit Model frame 81 x 35 cm
Base Camp Model frame 71 x 34 cm
Padded belts and shoulder straps

Send for
our catalogue

**P.O. Box 395
Florida 1710
Phone Johannesburg
673 5140
ask for Les Egling**

Leaders in outdoor living

x

MOUNTAIN SPLENDOUR
CARAVAN PARK

Come and join us in parklike surroundings. Sit and relax while gazing at the majestic Champagne Castle and Cathkin Peak. Savour the peace and quiet, or if you are in the mood, enjoy the pleasures of walking, hiking, picnicing, swimming and horseriding in this lovely valley. There is a golf course next door, and squash courts and bowling green nearby.
Once you have enjoyed the pleasures of our Park, you will want to return again and again.

For further information contact the owners:
Malcolm and Rea Don-Wauchope
P.O. Box 178, Winterton 3340
or Phone 03682 ask for 3503
WE LOOK FORWARD TO SEEING YOU

MOUNTAIN SPLENDOUR CARAVAN PARK

Set in the foothills of the Giants Castle area of the Drakensberg,
White Mountain Resort offers good home cooking, friendly
hospitality, comfortable rooms all with private bathroom
and carpeted. Wake up to a hearty breakfast served in the
Old Stone Trading Store, now a well appointed diningroom.
Have a game of bowls or tennis, then perhaps a refreshing
swim in our filtered pool. There are many glorious walks
and hikes to places of interest such as Fern Cave and
another cave where Bushmen once lived and left their
paintings amidst beautiful indigenous forests.
Horse rides are taken daily into the surrounding country side.
In the evening enjoy a friendly chat in the Old Stone Mill,
now a beautifully decorated Lounge.
Under the personal supervision of Angus and Lyn Clelland.

WHITE MOUNTAIN RESORT
THE GUEST FARM IN THE DRAKENSBERG

Ntabamhlope Natal

Phone Estcourt 24437   **P.O. Box 609, Estcourt (3310)**

EL MIRADOR HOTEL

P.O. Box Winterton 3340, Natal
Telephone:
03642 — Ask for El Mirador 3

EL MIRADOR : THE PLACE WITH A VIEW

From the gardens of this hotel, a panorama of the majestic Drakensberg stretches as far as the eye can see. A cool, clear river winds its way tranquilly through the valley.

Overlooking this beautiful valley rests our inter-denominational chapel. Instead of a stained glass window clear glass gives a magnificent view of some of the highest peaks in the Drakensberg. On the left is the inviting water of the sparkling swimming pool; on the right, two tennis courts and a match size bowling green. Behind is the Spanish-style hotel building fringed with delightful cottage-type rondavels.

Our conference centre is private and can seat up to 200 delegates. It is used for wedding receptions as well.

All this is set in lush lawns and flower gardens.

Our speciality is unusual bus tours to all parts of the Drakensberg and visits to Bushman paintings. Other amenities and include a squash court, billiards, table tennis, horse riding, evening entertainment and a nearby 9 hole golf course.

EL MIRADOR — FOR THE HOLIDAY YOU'VE ALWAYS WANTED.

Get a breath of fresh mountain air!

Take a break and get-away-from-it-all to

MONT AUX SOURCES HOTEL ★ TYYY

Drakensberg's most beautifully situated holiday resort.

A FRIENDLY SPOT

Bowls, tennis, swimming, horse riding, minature golf, organised walks and entertainments are yours to enjoy. We specialise in Bowls Tournaments.

Mont aux Sources Hotel
Private Bag 1
Mont aux Sources, 3353

Telephone 03642
ask for 7

DRAGON PEAKS PARK

The Caravaners and Campers holiday resort in the heart of the Drakensberg Mountains

Member of Club Caraville * Half Olympic size filtered and lighted
swimming pool with diving section * Billiard and TV room
Recreation and dance hall where movies and entertainment
are provided nightly in season * Riding, hiking, trout-fishing,
farm life, two modern ablution blocks with loads of hot water,
laundrette and trading store on site * 2 All weather competition
tennis courts * New tar road within 3 km * Golf course within 2 km
Shady sites and 10 with electric power * Cottages and Plettenbergs
for hire * Dams for yachting

TRY US! YOU WON'T FORGET US

Write to:
The Manager, Dragon Peaks Park, P.O. Winterton 3340, Natal
**Telephone: Bergville (03642) and ask for Dragon Peaks No. 1
between 08h00 and 17h00
After hours telephone (03682) and ask for 3713**